JESUS' LITTLE INSTRUCTION BOOK

JESUS' LITTLE INSTRUCTION BOOK

His Words to Your Heart

Compiled by Thomas Cahill

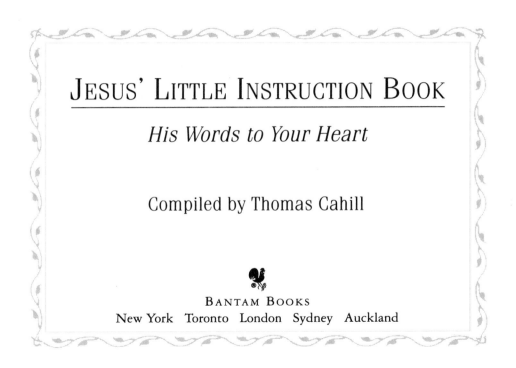

BANTAM BOOKS
New York   Toronto   London   Sydney   Auckland

JESUS' LITTLE INSTRUCTION BOOK
A Bantam Book / October 1994
All rights reserved.
Copyright © 1994 by Thomas Cahill
Translation of Philippians 2:6-11 by Thomas Cahill
All other translations from the New Testament are taken from *The New Jerusalem Bible*, copyright © 1985 by Doubleday,
a division of Bantam Doubleday Dell Publishing Group, Inc., and Darton, Longman & Todd, Ltd.
Used by permission of Doubleday.
Book design by Donna Sinisgalli
Library of Congress Cataloging-in-Publication Data
Bible. N.T. Gospels. English. New Jerusalem Bible. Selections. 1994.
Jesus' little instruction book : his words to your heart / compiled by Thomas Cahill.
p.   cm.
Words of Jesus from the Gospels of Matthew, Mark, and Luke.
ISBN 0-553-37433-8 (pbk.)
1. Jesus Christ—Words.   I. Cahill, Thomas.   II. Title.
BT306.C34 1994
226'.052076—dc20   94-15752
                                                    CIP
Published simultaneously in the United States and Canada

Bantam Books are published by Bantam Books, a division of Bantam Doubleday Dell Publishing Group, Inc. Its trademark,
consisting of the words "Bantam Books" and the portrayal of a rooster, is Registered in U.S. Patent and Trademark Office
and in other countries. Marca Registrada. Bantam Books, 1540 Broadway, New York, New York 10036.

PRINTED IN THE UNITED STATES OF AMERICA
0 9 8 7 6

*To Mario Marazziti and the Community of Sant'Egidio,
a genuine Gospel community, such as I had all but despaired of finding.*

CONTENTS

INTRODUCTION

So far as we know, Jesus never wrote anything down—or, if he did, nothing has survived. We are pretty sure he knew how to read and write. The gospels present him as reading aloud from the scroll of the scriptures in the synagogue; and, like other Jewish males of pious family, he would have been schooled as a child to read the Hebrew texts of Judaism's holy books.

But by Jesus' day, Hebrew was already a dead language, used principally in study and ritual. The day-to-day language of Jesus and his fellow Jews was Aramaic. The working language of the Roman conquerors who ruled over them was not Latin but Greek, which at that time served as an international language—as Latin would in the Middle Ages and as English does today. So Jesus probably knew some Greek as well, which would have been the language he used to respond to the questions of Pontius Pilate, the Roman procurator who condemned him to death.

Virtually all the sayings of Jesus that have come down to us are written in Greek, and most of these are contained in the four gospels of the New Testament. We know that few, if any, of these sayings can be verbatim, because the great bulk of what Jesus said he said in Aramaic. The Greek sayings of the gospels are translations of Jesus' original spoken words (and, as we read them *in English,* at one more remove from the originals). Furthermore, the gospel writers sometimes contradict one another—usually in minor details—by giving different versions of what Jesus said.

Before there were written gospels, there was human memory. Various participants in Jesus' life and witnesses to his spoken words joined the communities that formed "in his name" after his earthly life, and these people contributed their memories of him to the communal pool. One could almost say that memory was the central business of these groups. Informal and fairly unstructured, they met in one another's houses and tried to keep a low profile, since both Jews and Greeks were suspicious of them. At first, they called themselves followers of "the Way," a harmless-sounding phrase. To keep out spies, they used passwords and symbols and secret gestures. If you gained entrance to one of their meetings, you would have found yourself participating in a ritualized common meal at which a portion of the Jewish scriptures was read aloud and interpreted, a hymn was sung that explained the extraordinary significance the singers attached to Jesus' life, and bread and wine were distributed with the baffling admonition that these were to be consumed as "the body and blood" of Jesus himself.

Clearly, this "memorial service" to Jesus was more than an intellectual exercise. Memory of him had been joined to commitment—commitment to his Way, surely, but also to the astounding belief that he was still present among his followers, guiding them individually and animating their meeting. Some of the prayers and hymns of these primitive meetings (or "churches") have survived, embedded in the books of the New Testament, so we know how they sounded. One hymn, found in Paul's Letter to the Philippians, gives us a succinct summary of what the followers of the Way believed about Jesus:

Though he possessed divine estate
He was not jealous to retain
Equality with God.
He cast off his inheritance,
He took the nature of a slave
And walked as Man among men.
He emptied himself to the last
And was obedient to death—
To death upon a cross.
And, therefore, God has raised him up
And God has given him the Name-
Which-Is-Above-All-Names,
That at the Name of Jesus all
In heaven high shall bow the knee
And all the earth and depths
And every tongue of men proclaim
That Jesus Christ is LORD—
To the glory of the Father.

Though Jesus was divine, he had taken on our humanity, and had suffered and died for us, emptying himself "to the last." This total giving had resulted in his resurrection by the Father God and his exaltation as Lord of the Universe. So the followers of the Way kept the memory of his words and deeds, knowing that his was not the usual human story of life and suffering, ending in death. He was unique in all of history, a man whose life and works had been justified by the act of God himself, who had brought him back from the dead. It was because of this unique proof of the cosmic centrality of Jesus that they wished to remember everything they could about his earthly words and deeds.

But they had another reason for remembering. Jesus himself had urged them to "follow" him—to become like him. How could they? They did not come from God, they could not die on a cross for all humanity. But they could "empty" themselves, if not of blood, then of all pretension, all worldly ambition, all merely human striving. And they could remember his words and try to live their lives by them.

In this spirit, they began to make collections of his sayings. These collections, the need for which became more pressing as the generation of witnesses began to pass from the scene, were eventually joined to the oft-told story of Jesus' trial, execution, and miraculous resurrection to become written "go'spels" or "good spells"—that is, "good news." The earliest such gospel may be the Gospel According to Mark, probably committed to papyrus thirty-some years after Jesus' crucifixion, perhaps as a written equivalent of the teaching of Peter, the chief apostle. Or it may be that the apostle Matthew's Gospel was the first—in a primitive Aramaic version that we have lost. But each of the gospels has several, maybe many, parents. Just imagine all the elders who would have had a story or two to contribute! And when we imagine such interaction, we can easily see how, a full generation or more after the events of Jesus' life, some memories would be hard to square with others and some of the stories would have evolved over time to gain a richer meaning than they seemed once to possess. Such a process explains the minor discrepancies among the gospels of Matthew, Mark, and Luke. The Gospel According to John, on the other hand, seems to have been extensively rewritten more than once to make it relevant to the changing conditions (and crises) of the community that produced it. It may not have reached its final form until about the end of the first century.

What is far more remarkable than the inconsistencies and rewritings, however, is the consistent portrayal of the figure of Jesus. None of the evangelists (as the gospel authors are called) were practiced writers. Yet their words manage to convey a person, a human yet divine figure who reaches across the divide of twenty centuries to make direct contact with us. Because this troubling, uncanny, marvelous, healing contact has been experienced repeatedly by countless billions of human beings over two millennia, we may speak of the gospels as unique—books unlike any other books about a man unlike any other man, who lived a life that contains a mysterious message for each of us.

What follows is my collection of the words—and, on a couple of occasions, the silences—of Jesus as found in the four gospels. I have included only those sayings addressed to all and have omitted sayings that appear bound to particular historical circumstances (such as most of his instructions to the twelve apostles before their first mission in Chapter 10 of Matthew's Gospel). When the same (or similar) saying is found more than once, I have chosen one version. I have kept the sayings from the gospels of Matthew, Mark, and Luke together and gathered the distinctive sayings from John's Gospel into a separate section.

If you read these sayings in sequence, you may find that they are not especially sequential. Neither Jesus nor the gospel writers kept to the strict "first this, then that" logic that we are accustomed to. The progress of Jesus' thought is more like a spiral than a straight line. He tends to say the same things again and again. But with each repetition there is a new twist. As you follow him through his story, you can see that he begins by interacting mainly with large groups of people, painting his program with broad brush strokes at first, and gradually concentrating his attention on smaller groups of friends and enemies. As he becomes more and more pointed in his instructions, his enemies become more fierce, vocal, and dark minded, and his friends more loyal, committed, and enlightened. It is as if the gospels started with the undifferentiated mass of humanity, which gradually separates itself out into good and evil poles in response to the figure of Jesus—and all in preparation for the final conflict, with its cosmic implications.

The translation I have used is *The New Testament of The New Jerusalem Bible,* hardly the most famous or most used translation, but to my ear the most noble *and* contemporary. It is also, so far as I can judge, extremely accurate. Its notes and introductions are both reader friendly and profound, and I heartily recommend it to all who come to enjoy these excerpts.

Do not read *Jesus' Little Instruction Book* all at once. Savor what you read. Go on only when you have sucked all the goodness out of each saying. There is nothing to be afraid of here. Open this book and let him speak to you, as if for the first time, whom you have always wanted to hear, whether you knew it or not.

JESUS' LITTLE INSTRUCTION BOOK

THE WORDS OF JESUS

From the Gospels of Matthew, Mark, and Luke

JESUS INVITES YOU

"Repent, for the kingdom of Heaven is close at hand."

MATTHEW 4:17

As he was walking by the Lake of Galilee he saw two brothers, Simon, who was called Peter, and his brother Andrew; they were making a cast into the lake with their net, for they were fishermen. And he said to them, "Come after me and I will make you fishers of people." And at once they left their nets and followed him.

MATTHEW 4:18–20

The Bible is actually a collection of books, with each book divided into chapters and verses. Thus "Matthew" (or "Matt." or "Mt") is a book of the Bible titled "The Gospel According to Matthew"; "4" is "Chapter 4"; and "18–20" are "verses 18

3

through 20." The Bible is divided into two great sections: the Old Testament, which is a collection of the sacred scriptures of the Jews, and the New Testament, of which the gospels make up the first four books.

JESUS' BASIC PROGRAM

THE BEATITUDES

"How blessed are the poor in spirit:
the kingdom of Heaven is theirs.
Blessed are *the gentle:*
they shall have the earth as inheritance.
Blessed are those who mourn:
they shall be comforted.
Blessed are those who hunger and thirst for uprightness:
they shall have their fill.
Blessed are the merciful:
they shall have mercy shown them.

Blessed are the pure in heart:
they shall see God.
Blessed are the peacemakers:
they shall be recognized as children of God.
Blessed are those who are persecuted in the cause of uprightness:
the kingdom of Heaven is theirs.
Blessed are you when people abuse you and persecute you and
speak all kinds of calumny against you falsely on my account.
Rejoice and be glad, for your reward will be great in heaven; this
is how they persecuted the prophets before you."

MATTHEW 5:3–12

These sayings are called "Beatitudes," after "beati," the Latin word for blessed,
which Jerome used when he translated the original Greek gospels into Latin in the
late fourth century. His translation of the Bible, called the Vulgate (or common) ver-
sion, remained the standard in the West for more than a thousand years—until the
6 *translations into the European vernacular languages during the Reformation period.*

The Beatitudes are the beginning of what is usually called "The Sermon on the Mount" (Matthew 5–7), which is really just Matthew's arrangement of a more primitive collection of Jesus' sayings.

Whenever Jesus quotes from the Jewish scriptures, his words are set in italics.

YOU ARE SALT

> "You are salt for the earth. But if salt loses its taste, what can make it salty again? It is good for nothing, and can only be thrown out to be trampled under people's feet."
>
> MATTHEW 5:13

YOU ARE LIGHT

"You are light for the world. A city built on a hill-top cannot be hidden. No one lights a lamp to put it under a tub; they put it on the lamp-stand where it shines for everyone in the house. In the same way your light must shine in people's sight, so that, seeing your good works, they may give praise to your Father in heaven."

MATTHEW 5:14–16

JESUS THE JEW

"Do not imagine that I have come to abolish the Law or the Prophets. I have come not to abolish but to complete them. In truth I tell you, till heaven and earth disappear, not one dot, not one little stroke, is to disappear from the Law until all its purpose is achieved. Therefore, anyone who infringes even one of the least of these commandments and teaches others to do the same will be considered the least in the kingdom of Heaven; but the person who keeps them and teaches them will be considered great in the kingdom of Heaven."

MATTHEW 5:17–19

The Law (or Torah) refers to the first five books of the sacred scriptures of the Jews, which contain a series of laws, and most important the Ten Commandments. But, more deeply, the Law refers to the attitudes toward life to be found in these books. The Prophets are the books of the Jewish scriptures that contain the words of men recognized as prophets, like Isaiah and Jeremiah, who recall the Jews to their own highest moral standards. "The Law and the Prophets" together form the most revered part of the Jewish canon, or definitive group of sacred writings.

Jesus then urges us to fulfill God's commandments, not by legalistic nitpicking, but by a truly interior response:

> "For I tell you, if your uprightness does not surpass that of the scribes and Pharisees, you will never get into the kingdom of Heaven."
>
> MATTHEW 5:20

Pharisees were rabbis who belonged to a reform movement that had begun prior to Jesus' day and that stressed strict observance of all the details of the Jewish Law. By Jesus' time, this movement may have become corrupt or at least begun to harbor corrupt members. But such a characterization is based on little more than speculation. All we can say for sure is that Jesus had such a low opinion of them that the name Pharisee became synonymous with hypocrite. This portrayal of the Pharisees has unfortunately

also figured in Christian prejudice against Jews, which Jesus the Jew would hardly have intended. See page 104 for additional interpretation.

DON'T HURT OTHERS

"You have heard how it was said to our ancestors, *You shall not kill;* and if anyone does kill he must answer for it before the court. But I say this to you, anyone who is angry with a brother will answer for it before the court; anyone who calls a brother 'Fool' will answer for it before the Sanhedrin; and anyone who calls him 'Traitor' will answer for it in hell fire. So then, if you are bringing your offering to the altar and there remember that your brother has something against you, leave your offering there before the altar, go and be reconciled with your brother first, and then come back and present your offering. Come to terms with your opponent in good time while you are still on the way to the court with him, or he may hand you over to the judge and the judge to the officer, and you will be thrown into

11

prison. In truth I tell you, you will not get out till you have
paid the last penny."

MATTHEW 5:21–26

*The Sanhedrin was the high court in Jerusalem, before which Jesus himself would
eventually be brought.*

BE FAITHFUL IN YOUR HEART

"You have heard how it was said, *You shall not commit adultery.* But
I say this to you, if a man looks at a woman lustfully, he has
already committed adultery with her in his heart. If your right
eye should be your downfall, tear it out and throw it away; for it
will do you less harm to lose one part of yourself than to have
your whole body thrown into hell. And if your right hand should
be your downfall, cut it off and throw it away; for it will do you

less harm to lose one part of yourself than to have your whole body go to hell."

MATTHEW 5:27–30

LET'S HAVE ONE STANDARD FOR MEN AND WOMEN

"It has also been said, *Anyone who divorces his wife must give her a writ of dismissal.* But I say this to you, everyone who divorces his wife, except for the case of an illicit marriage, makes her an adulteress; and anyone who marries a divorced woman commits adultery."

MATTHEW 5:31–32

According to the Law, a man could obtain a divorce even for a trivial reason, but a woman could not obtain a divorce. Jesus, rejecting this double standard, insists that men and women be bound equally.

SPEAK PLAINLY

"Again, you have heard how it was said to our ancestors, *You must not break your oath, but must fulfill your oaths to the Lord.* But I say this to you, do not swear at all, either by *heaven,* since that is *God's throne;* or by *earth,* since that is *his footstool;* or by Jerusalem, since that is *the city of the great King.* Do not swear by your own head either, since you cannot turn a single hair white or black. All you need say is 'Yes' if you mean yes, 'No' if you mean no; anything more than this comes from the Evil One."

MATTHEW 5:33–37

GO THE EXTRA MILE

"You have heard how it was said: *Eye for eye and tooth for tooth.* But I say this to you: offer no resistance to the wicked. On the contrary, if anyone hits you on the right cheek, offer him the other as well; if someone wishes to go to law with you to get your tunic, let him have your cloak as well. And if anyone requires you to go one mile, go two miles with him. Give to anyone who asks you, and if anyone wants to borrow, do not turn away."

MATTHEW 5:38–42

LOVE AS THE FATHER LOVES

"You have heard how it was said, *You will love your neighbor* and hate your enemy. But I say this to you, love your enemies and pray for those who persecute you; so that you may be children of your Father in heaven, for he causes his sun to rise on the bad as well as the good, and sends down rain to fall on the upright and the wicked alike. For if you love those who love you, what reward will you get? Do not even the tax collectors do as much? And if you save your greetings for your brothers, are you doing anything exceptional? Do not even the gentiles do as much? You must therefore set no bounds to your love, just as your heavenly Father sets none to his."

MATTHEW 5:43–48

Gentiles are non-Jews—all the other "nations" (or ethnic groupings) of the world.

GIVE IN SECRET

"Be careful not to parade your uprightness in public to attract attention; otherwise you will lose all reward from your Father in heaven. So when you give alms, do not have it trumpeted before you; this is what the hypocrites do in the synagogues and in the streets to win human admiration. In truth I tell you, they have had their reward. But when you give alms, your left hand must not know what your right is doing; your almsgiving must be secret, and your Father who sees all that is done in secret will reward you."

MATTHEW 6:1–4

PRAY IN SECRET

"And when you pray, do not imitate the hypocrites: they love to say their prayers standing up in the synagogues and at the street corners for people to see them. In truth I tell you, they have had their reward. But when you pray, *go to your private room, shut yourself in, and so pray* to your Father who is in that secret place, and your Father who sees all that is done in secret will reward you."

MATTHEW 6:5–6

"In your prayers do not babble as the gentiles do, for they think that by using many words they will make themselves heard. Do not be like them; your Father knows what you need before you ask him. So you should pray like this:

Our Father in heaven,
may your name be held holy,
your kingdom come,
your will be done,
on earth as in heaven.
Give us today our daily bread.
And forgive us our debts,
as we have forgiven those who are in debt to us.
And do not put us to the test,
but save us from the Evil One."

18

MATTHEW 6:7–13

Called The Lord's Prayer, these words of Jesus are meant to encourage us to spontaneous, heartfelt prayer. The last thing he intended was for us to consecrate his words and make them unchangeable.

HOW TO BE FORGIVEN

> "Yes, if you forgive others their failings, your heavenly Father will forgive you yours; but if you do not forgive others, your Father will not forgive your failings either."
>
> MATTHEW 6:14–15

FAST IN SECRET

> "When you are fasting, do not put on a gloomy look as the hypocrites do: they go about looking unsightly to let people know they are fasting. In truth I tell you, they have had their reward. But when you fast, put scent on your head and wash your

19

face, so that no one will know you are fasting except your Father who sees all that is done in secret; and your Father who sees all that is done in secret will reward you."

MATTHEW 6:16–18

WHERE IS YOUR HEART?

"Do not store up treasures for yourselves on earth, where moth and woodworm destroy them and thieves can break in and steal. But store up treasures for yourselves in heaven, where neither moth nor woodworm destroys them and thieves cannot break in and steal. For wherever your treasure is, there will your heart be too."

MATTHEW 6:19–21

THE BODY'S LIGHT

"The lamp of the body is the eye. It follows that if your eye is clear, your whole body will be filled with light. But if your eye is diseased, your whole body will be darkness. If then, the light inside you is darkened, what darkness that will be!"

MATTHEW 6:22–23

GOD OR MONEY

"No one can be the slave of two masters: he will either hate the first and love the second, or be attached to the first and despise the second. You cannot be the slave both of God and of money."

MATTHEW 6:24

"That is why I am telling you not to worry about your life and what you are to eat, nor about your body and what you are to wear. Surely life is more than food, and the body more than clothing! Look at the birds in the sky. They do not sow or reap or gather into barns; yet your heavenly Father feeds them. Are you not worth much more than they are? Can any of you, however much you worry, add one single cubit to your span of life? And why worry about clothing? Think of the flowers growing in the fields; they never have to work or spin; yet I assure you that not even Solomon in all his royal robes was clothed like one of these. Now if that is how God clothes the wild flowers growing in the field which are there today and thrown into the furnace tomorrow, will he not much more look after you, you who have so little faith? So do not worry; do not say, 'What are we to eat? What are we to drink? What are we to wear?' It is the gentiles who set their hearts on all these things. Your heavenly Father knows you need them all. Set your hearts on his kingdom first, and on God's saving justice, and all these other things will be given you as well. So do not worry about tomorrow: tomorrow will take care of itself. Each day has enough trouble of its own."

MATTHEW 6:25–34

Solomon was the son of King David and legendary for his grandeur.

DON'T JUDGE OTHERS

"Do not judge, and you will not be judged; because the judgments you give are the judgments you will get, and the standard you use will be the standard used for you. Why do you observe the splinter in your brother's eye and never notice the great log in your own? And how dare you say to your brother, 'Let me take that splinter out of your eye,' when, look, there is a great log in your own? Hypocrite! Take the log out of your own

23

eye first, and then you will see clearly enough to take the splinter out of your brother's eye."

MATTHEW 7:1–5

CHERISH HOLY THINGS

"Do not give dogs what is holy; and do not throw your pearls in front of pigs, or they may trample them and then turn on you and tear you to pieces."

MATTHEW 7:6

ASK AS A CHILD ASKS

"Ask, and it will be given to you; search, and you will find; knock, and the door will be opened to you. Everyone who asks receives; everyone who searches finds; everyone who knocks will have the door opened. Is there anyone among you who would hand his son a stone when he asked for bread? Or would hand him a snake when he asked for a fish? If you, then, evil as you are, know how to give your children what is good, how much more will your Father in heaven give good things to those who ask him!"

MATTHEW 7:7–11

THE GOLDEN RULE

"Always treat others as you would like them to treat you; that is the Law and the Prophets."

MATTHEW 7:12

THE TWO ROADS

"Enter by the narrow gate, since the road that leads to destruction
is wide and spacious, and many take it; but it is a narrow gate
and a hard road that leads to life, and only a few find it."

MATTHEW 7:13–14

BEWARE OF WOLVES IN SHEEP'S CLOTHING

"Beware of false prophets who come to you disguised as sheep but
underneath are ravenous wolves. You will be able to tell them
by their fruits. Can people pick grapes from thorns, or figs from
thistles? In the same way, a sound tree produces good fruit but a
rotten tree bad fruit. A sound tree cannot bear bad fruit, nor a
rotten tree bear good fruit. Any tree that does not produce good

fruit is cut down and thrown on the fire. I repeat, you will be able to tell them by their fruits."

MATTHEW 7:15–20

DO GOD'S WILL

"It is not anyone who says to me, 'Lord, Lord,' who will enter the kingdom of Heaven, but the person who does the will of my Father in heaven. When the day comes many will say to me, 'Lord, Lord, did we not prophesy in your name, drive out demons in your name, work many miracles in your name?' Then I shall tell them to their faces: I have never known you; *away from me, all evil doers!*

"Therefore, everyone who listens to these words of mine and acts on them will be like a sensible man who built his house on rock. Rain came down, floods rose, gales blew and hurled themselves against that house, and it did not fall: it was founded on rock. But everyone who listens to these words of mine and does not act on them will be like a stupid man who built his house on sand. Rain came down, floods rose, gales blew and struck that house, and it fell; and what a fall it had!"

MATTHEW 7:21–27

JESUS' MISSION—AND OURS

FAITH HEALS

A centurion . . . had a servant, a favorite of his, who was sick and near death. Having heard about Jesus he sent some Jewish elders to him to ask him to come and heal his servant. . . . So Jesus went with them, and was not very far from the house when the centurion sent word to him by some friends to say to him, "Sir, do not put yourself to any trouble because I am not worthy to have you under my roof; and that is why I did not presume to come to you myself; let my boy be cured by your giving the word. For I am under authority myself, and have soldiers under me; and I say to one man, 'Go,' and he goes; to another, 'Come here,' and he

comes; to my servant, 'Do this,' and he does it." When Jesus
heard these words he was astonished at him and, turning round,
said to the crowd following him, "I tell you, not even in Israel
have I found faith as great as this." And when the messengers got
back to the house they found the servant in perfect health.

LUKE 7:2–10

THE COST OF DISCIPLESHIP

As they traveled along they met a man on the road who said to
him, "I will follow you wherever you go." Jesus answered, "Foxes
have holes and the birds of the air have nests, but the Son of man
has nowhere to lay his head."

Another to whom he said, "Follow me," replied, "Let me go
and bury my father first." But he answered, "Leave the dead to

bury their dead; your duty is to go and spread the news of the kingdom of God."

LUKE 9:57–60

THE FAITH OF JESUS

Then he got into the boat followed by his disciples. Suddenly a storm broke over the lake, so violent that the boat was being swamped by the waves. But he was asleep. So they went to him and woke him saying, "Save us, Lord, we are lost!" And he said to them, "Why are you so frightened, you who have so little faith?" And then he stood up and rebuked the winds and the sea; and there was a great calm. They were astounded and said, "Whatever kind of man is this, that even the winds and the sea obey him?"

MATTHEW 8:23–27

WHO CAN FORGIVE SINS?

Some people came bringing him a paralytic carried by four men, but as they could not get the man to him through the crowd, they stripped the roof over the place where Jesus was; and when they had made an opening, they lowered the stretcher on which the paralytic lay. Seeing their faith, Jesus said to the paralytic, "My child, your sins are forgiven." Now some scribes were sitting there, and they thought to themselves, "How can this man talk like that? He is being blasphemous. Who but God can forgive sins?" And at once, Jesus, inwardly aware that this is what they were thinking, said to them, "Why do you have these thoughts in your hearts? Which of these is easier to say to the paralytic, 'Your sins are forgiven' or to say, 'Get up, pick up your stretcher and walk?' But to prove to you that the Son of man has authority to forgive sins on earth"—he said to the paralytic—"I order you: get up, pick up your stretcher, and go off home." And the man got up, and at once picked up his stretcher and walked out in front of everyone, so that they were all astonished and praised God saying, "We have never seen anything like this."

MARK 2:3–12

JESUS' TABLE FELLOWSHIP

Now while he was at table in the house it happened that a number of tax collectors and sinners came to sit at the table with Jesus and his disciples. When the Pharisees saw this, they said to his disciples, "Why does your master eat with tax collectors and sinners?" When he heard this he replied, "It is not the healthy who need the doctor, but the sick. Go and learn the meaning of the words: *Mercy is what pleases me, not sacrifice.* And indeed I came to call not the upright, but sinners."

MATTHEW 9:10–13

ENJOY THE FEAST WHILE IT LASTS

Then John's disciples came to him and said, "Why is it that we and the Pharisees fast, but your disciples do not?" Jesus replied, "Surely the bridegroom's attendants cannot mourn as long as the bridegroom is still with them? But the time will come when the bridegroom is taken away from them, and then they will fast."

MATTHEW 9:14–15

YOUR WORTH

"Do not be afraid of those who kill the body but cannot kill the soul; fear him rather who can destroy both body and soul in hell. Can you not buy two sparrows for a penny? And yet not one falls to the ground without your Father knowing. Why, every hair on your head has been counted. So there is no need to be afraid; you are worth more than many sparrows."

MATTHEW 10:28–31

THE INTERSECTION OF HEAVEN AND EARTH

"So if anyone declares himself for me in the presence of human beings, I will declare myself for him in the presence of my Father in heaven. But the one who disowns me in the presence of human beings, I will disown in the presence of my Father in heaven."

MATTHEW 10:32–33

JESUS' FOLLOWERS SHOULD NOT EXPECT PEACE

"Do not suppose that I have come to bring peace to the earth: it is not peace I have come to bring, but a sword. For I have come to set son against *father, daughter against mother, daughter-in-law against mother-in-law; a person's enemies will be the members of his own household."*

MATTHEW 10:34–36

HUMAN TIES COME SECOND

"No one who prefers father or mother to me is worthy of me. No one who prefers son or daughter to me is worthy of me. Anyone who does not take his cross and follow in my footsteps is not worthy of me. Anyone who finds his life will lose it; anyone who loses his life for my sake will find it."

MATTHEW 10:37–39

THE HIDDEN KNOWLEDGE—AND THOSE WHO POSSESS IT

"I bless you, Father, Lord of heaven and of earth, for hiding these things from the learned and the clever and revealing them to little children. Yes, Father, for that is what it pleased you to do. Everything has been entrusted to me by my Father; and no one knows the Son except the Father, just as no one knows the Father except the Son and those to whom the Son chooses to reveal him."

MATTHEW 11:25–27

COMFORT FOR THOSE WHO ARE WEIGHED DOWN

"Come to me, all you who labor and are overburdened, and I will give you rest. Shoulder my yoke and learn from me, for I am gentle and humble in heart, *and you will find rest for your souls.* Yes, my yoke is easy and my burden light."

MATTHEW 11:28–30

A WARNING TO THE RICH AND SELF-SATISFIED

"But alas for you who are rich: you are having your
consolation now.
Alas for you who have plenty to eat now: you shall go
hungry.
Alas for you who are laughing now: you shall mourn
and weep.
Alas for you when everyone speaks well of you! This was the way
their ancestors treated the false prophets."

LUKE 6:24–26

GENEROSITY

"If you lend to those from whom you hope to get money back,
what credit can you expect? Even sinners lend to sinners to get
back the same amount. Instead, love your enemies and do good to

them, and lend without any hope of return. You will have a great reward, and you will be children of the Most High, for he himself is kind to the ungrateful and the wicked.

"Be compassionate just as your Father is compassionate. Do not judge, and you will not be judged; do not condemn, and you will not be condemned; forgive, and you will be forgiven. Give, and there will be gifts for you: a full measure, pressed down, shaken together, and overflowing, will be poured into your lap; because the standard you use will be the standard used for you."

LUKE 6:34–38

THE WOMAN WHO LOVED MUCH

One of the Pharisees invited him to a meal. When he arrived at the Pharisee's house and took his place at table, suddenly a woman came in, who had a bad name in the town. She had heard he was dining with the Pharisee and had brought with her an alabaster jar of ointment. She waited behind him at his feet, weeping, and her tears fell on his feet, and she wiped them away with her hair; then she covered his feet with kisses and anointed them with the ointment.

When the Pharisee who had invited him saw this, he said to himself, "If this man were a prophet, he would know who this woman is and what sort of person it is who is touching him and what a bad name she has." Then Jesus took him up and said, "Simon, I have something to say to you." He replied, "Say on, Master." "There was once a creditor who had two men in his debt; one owed him five hundred denarii, the other fifty. They were unable to pay, so he let them both off. Which of them will love him more?" Simon answered, "The one who was let off more, I suppose." Jesus said, "You are right."

Then he turned to the woman and said to Simon, "You see this woman? I came into your house, and you poured no water over my feet, but she has poured out her tears over my feet and wiped them away with her hair. You gave me no kiss, but she has been covering my feet with kisses ever since I came in. You did not anoint my head with oil, but she has anointed my feet with ointment. For this reason I tell you that her sins, many as they are, have been forgiven her, because she has shown such great love. It is someone who is forgiven little who shows little love." Then he said to her, "Your sins are forgiven." Those who were with him at table began to say to themselves, "Who is this man, that even forgives sins?" But he said to the woman, "Your faith has saved you; go in peace."

LUKE 7:36–50

YOU CANNOT CONQUER EVIL IN EVIL'S NAME

"Every kingdom divided against itself is heading for ruin; and no town, no household divided against itself can last. Now if Satan drives out Satan, he is divided against himself; so how can his kingdom last? And if it is through Beelzebub that I drive devils out, through whom do your own experts drive them out? They shall be your judges, then. But if it is through the Spirit of God that I drive out devils, then be sure that the kingdom of God has caught you unawares.

"Or again, how can anyone make his way into a strong man's house and plunder his property unless he has first tied up the strong man? Only then can he plunder his house.

"Anyone who is not with me is against me, and anyone who does not gather in with me throws away. And so I tell you, every human sin and blasphemy will be forgiven, but blasphemy against the Spirit will not be forgiven. And anyone who says a word against the Son of man will be forgiven; but no one who speaks against the Holy Spirit will be forgiven either in this world or in the next."

MATTHEW 12:25–32

42   *Beelzebub is the name of a demon.*

KINSHIP WITH JESUS

Now his mother and his brothers arrived and, standing outside, sent in a message asking for him. A crowd was sitting round him at the time the message was passed to him, "Look, your mother and brothers and sisters are outside asking for you." He replied, "Who are my mother and my brothers?" And looking at those sitting in a circle round him, he said, "Here are my mother and my brothers. Anyone who does the will of God, that person is my brother and sister and mother."

MARK 3:31–35

THE SOWER AND HIS SEEDS

"Listen! Imagine a sower going out to sow. Now it happened that, as he sowed, some of the seed fell on the edge of the path, and the birds came and ate it up. Some seed fell on rocky ground

43

where it found little soil and at once sprang up, because there was no depth of earth; and when the sun came up it was scorched and, not having any roots, it withered away. Some seed fell into thorns, and the thorns grew up and choked it, and it produced no crop. And some seeds fell into rich soil, grew tall and strong, and produced a good crop; the yield was thirty, sixty, even a hundredfold. . . . Anyone who has ears for listening should listen!

"What the sower is sowing is the word. Those on the edge of the path where the word is sown are people who have no sooner heard it than Satan at once comes and carries away the word that was sown in them. Similarly, those who are sown on patches of rock are people who, when first they hear the word, welcome it at once with joy. But they have no root deep down and do not last; should some trial come, or some persecution on account of the word, at once they fall away. Then there are others who are sown in thorns. These have heard the word, but the worries of the world, the lure of riches and all the other passions come in to choke the word, and so it produces nothing. And there are those who have been sown in rich soil; they hear the word and accept it and yield a harvest, thirty and sixty and a hundredfold."

MARK 4:3–9; 13–20

WHAT THE KINGDOM IS LIKE

"This is what the kingdom of God is like. A man scatters seed on the land. Night and day, while he sleeps, when he is awake, the seed is sprouting and growing; how, he does not know. Of its own accord the land produces first the shoot, then the ear, then the full grain in the ear. And when the crop is ready, at once he starts to reap because the harvest has come."

MARK 4:26–29

"The kingdom of Heaven may be compared to a man who sowed good seed in his field. While everybody was asleep his enemy came, sowed darnel all among the wheat, and made off. When the new wheat sprouted and ripened, then the darnel appeared as well. The owner's laborers went to him and said, 'Sir, was it not good seed that you sowed in your field? If so, where does the darnel come from?' He said to them, 'Some enemy has done this.' And the laborers said, 'Do you want us to go and weed it out?' But he said, 'No, because when you weed out the darnel you might pull up the wheat with it. Let them both grow till the harvest; and at harvest time I shall say to the reapers: First collect the darnel and tie it in bundles to be burnt, then gather the wheat into my barn.'

"The sower of the good seed is the Son of man. The field is the world; the good seed is the subjects of the kingdom; the darnel, the subjects of the Evil One; the enemy who sowed it, the devil; the harvest is the end of the world; the reapers are the angels. Well then, just as the darnel is gathered up and burnt in the fire, so it will be at the end of time. The Son of man will send his angels and they will gather out of his kingdom all causes of falling and all who do evil, and throw them into the blazing furnace, where there will be weeping and grinding of teeth. Then the upright will shine like the sun in the kingdom of their Father. Anyone who has ears should listen!"

MATTHEW 13:24–30;
38–43

"The kingdom of Heaven is like a mustard seed which a man took and sowed in his field. It is the smallest of all the seeds, but when it has grown it is the biggest of shrubs and becomes a tree, so that the birds of the air can come and shelter in its branches."

MATTHEW 13:31–32

"The kingdom of Heaven is like the yeast a woman took and mixed in with three measures of flour till it was leavened all through."

MATTHEW 13:33

"The kingdom of Heaven is like treasure hidden in a field which someone has found; he hides it again, goes off in his joy, sells everything he owns and buys the field."

MATTHEW 13:44

"Again, the kingdom of Heaven is like a merchant looking for fine pearls; when he finds one of great value he goes and sells everything he owns and buys it."

MATTHEW 13:45–46

"Again, the kingdom of Heaven is like a dragnet that is cast in the sea and brings in a haul of all kinds of fish. When it is full, the fishermen haul it ashore; then, sitting down, they collect the good ones in baskets and throw away those that are no use. This is how it will be at the end of time: the angels will appear and separate the wicked from the upright, to throw them into the blazing furnace, where there will be weeping and grinding of teeth."

MATTHEW 13:47–50

JESUS WITH OTHERS

JESUS IGNORES JEWISH CUSTOM . . .

Then Pharisees and scribes from Jerusalem came to Jesus and said, "Why do your disciples break away from the tradition of the elders? They eat without washing their hands." He answered, "And why do you break away from the commandment of God for the sake of your tradition? For God said, *'Honor your father and your mother'* and *'Anyone who curses his father or mother will be put to death.'* But you say, 'If anyone says to his father or mother: Anything I might have used to help you is dedicated to God, he is rid of his duty to father or mother.' In this way you have made God's word ineffective by means of your tradition.

49

Hypocrites! How rightly Isaiah prophesied about you when he said:

This people honors me only with lip-service,
while their hearts are far from me.
Their reverence of me is worthless;
the lessons they teach are nothing but human
   commandments."

He called the people to him and said, "Listen, and understand. What goes into the mouth does not make anyone unclean; it is what comes out of the mouth that makes someone unclean."

MATTHEW 15:1–11

Then the disciples came to him and said, "Do you know that the Pharisees were shocked when they heard what you said?" He replied, "Any plant my heavenly Father has not planted will be pulled up by the roots. Leave them alone. They are blind leaders of the blind; and if one blind person leads another, both will fall into a pit."

At this, Peter said to him, "Explain the parable for us." Jesus replied, "Even you—don't you yet understand? Can't you see that whatever goes into the mouth passes through the stomach and is discharged into the sewer? But whatever comes out of the mouth comes from the heart, and it is this that makes someone unclean. For from the heart come evil intentions: murder, adultery, fornication, theft, perjury, slander. These are the things that make a person unclean. But eating with unwashed hands does not make anyone unclean."

MATTHEW 15:12–20   **51**

THE LEAVEN OF THE PHARISEES

The disciples, having crossed to the other side, had forgotten to take any food. Jesus said to them, "Keep your eyes open, and be on your guard against the yeast of the Pharisees and Sadducees." And they said among themselves, "It is because we have not brought any bread." Jesus knew it, and he said, "You have so little faith, why are you talking among yourselves about having no bread? Do you still not understand? Do you not remember the five loaves for the five thousand and the number of baskets you collected? Or the seven loaves for the four thousand and the number of baskets you collected? How could you fail to understand that I was not talking about bread? What I said was: Beware of the yeast of the Pharisees and Sadducees." Then they understood that he was telling them to be on their guard, not against yeast for making bread, but against the teaching of the Pharisees and Sadducees.

MATTHEW 16:5–12

JESUS CONFIRMS PETER

Jesus put this question to his disciples, "Who do people say the Son of man is?" And they said, "Some say John the Baptist, some Elijah, and others Jeremiah or one of the prophets." "But you," he said, "who do you say I am?" Then Simon Peter spoke up and said, "You are the Christ, the Son of the living God." Jesus replied, "Simon son of Jonah, you are a blessed man! Because it was no human agency that revealed this to you but my Father in heaven. So I now say to you: You are Peter and on this rock I will build my community. And the gates of the underworld can never overpower it. I will give you the keys of the kingdom of Heaven: whatever you bind on earth will be bound in heaven; whatever you loose on earth will be loosed in heaven."

MATTHEW 16:13–19

53

Christ is an Englishing of "Christos," the Greek word for "Anointed One"—that is, the promised Jewish Messiah, anointed (or designated) by God to liberate God's people.

JESUS REJECTS PETER

From then onwards Jesus began to make it clear to his disciples that he was destined to go to Jerusalem and suffer grievously at the hands of the elders and chief priests and scribes and to be put to death and to be raised up on the third day. Then, taking him aside, Peter started to rebuke him. "Heaven preserve you, Lord," he said, "this must not happen to you." But he turned and said to Peter, "Get behind me, Satan! You are an obstacle in my path, because you are thinking not as God thinks but as human beings do."

MATTHEW 16:21–23

Jesus took with him Peter and James and his brother John and led them up a high mountain by themselves. There in their presence he was transfigured: his face shone like the sun and his clothes became as dazzling as light. And suddenly Moses and Elijah appeared to them; they were talking with him. Then Peter spoke to Jesus. "Lord," he said, "it is wonderful for us to be here; if you want me to, I will make three shelters here, one for you, one for Moses and one for Elijah." He was still speaking when suddenly a bright cloud covered them with shadow, and suddenly from the cloud there came a voice which said, "This is my Son, the Beloved; he enjoys my favor. Listen to him." When they heard this, the disciples fell on their faces, overcome with fear. But Jesus came up and touched them, saying, "Stand up, do not be afraid." And when they raised their eyes they saw no one but Jesus.

MATTHEW 17:1–8

JESUS AGAIN PREDICTS THE FUTURE

When they were together in Galilee, Jesus said to them, "The Son of man is going to be delivered into the power of men; they will put him to death, and on the third day he will be raised up again." And a great sadness came over them.

MATTHEW 17:22–23

WHO IS THE GREATEST?

The disciples came to Jesus and said, "Who is the greatest in the kingdom of Heaven?" So he called a little child to him whom he set among them. Then he said, "In truth I tell you,

unless you change and become like little children you will
never enter the kingdom of Heaven. And so, the one who
makes himself as little as this little child is the greatest in the
kingdom of Heaven."

MATTHEW 18:1–4

WHO IS A CHRISTIAN?

John said to him, "Master, we saw someone who is not one of us
driving out devils in your name, and because he was not one of us
we tried to stop him." But Jesus said, "You must not stop him;
no one who works a miracle in my name could soon afterward
speak evil of me. Anyone who is not against us is for us.

"If anyone gives you a cup of water to drink because you
belong to Christ, then in truth I tell you, he will most certainly
not lose his reward."

MARK 9:38–41

JESUS INSTRUCTS HIS FRIENDS

CHERISH CHILDREN

"Anyone who welcomes one little child like this in my name
welcomes me. But anyone who is the downfall of one of these little
ones who have faith in me would be better drowned in the depths
of the sea with a great millstone round his neck. Alas for the world
that there should be such causes of falling! Causes of falling indeed
there must be, but alas for anyone who provides them! . . .

"See that you never despise any of these little ones, for I tell
you that their angels in heaven are continually in the presence of
my Father in heaven."

58

MATTHEW 18:5–7; 10

THE LOST SHEEP

"Which one of you with a hundred sheep, if he lost one, would
fail to leave the ninety-nine in the desert and go after the missing
one till he found it? And when he found it, would he not joyfully
take it on his shoulders and then, when he got home, call together
his friends and neighbors saying to them, 'Rejoice with me, I
have found my sheep that was lost.' In the same way, I tell you,
there will be more rejoicing in heaven over one sinner repenting
than over ninety-nine upright people who have no need of
repentance."

LUKE 15:4–7

HOW TO CORRECT A BROTHER

"If your brother does something wrong, go and have it out with
him alone, between your two selves. If he listens to you, you have

won back your brother. If he does not listen, take one or two others along with you: *whatever the misdemeanor, the evidence of two or three witnesses is required to sustain the charge.* But if he refuses to listen to these, report it to the community; and if he refuses to listen to the community, treat him like a gentile or a tax collector.

"In truth I tell you, whatever you bind on earth will be bound in heaven: whatever you loose on earth will be loosed in heaven."

MATTHEW 18:15–18

COMMON PRAYER

"In truth I tell you once again, if two of you on earth agree to ask anything at all, it will be granted to you by my Father in heaven. For where two or three meet in my name, I am there among them."

60

MATTHEW 18:19–20

HOW OFTEN MUST I FORGIVE?

Then Peter went up to him and said, "Lord, how often must I
forgive my brother if he wrongs me? As often as seven times?"
Jesus answered, "Not seven, I tell you, but seventy-seven times."

MATTHEW 18:21–22

HARDNESS OF HEART HAS ITS CONSEQUENCES

"And so the kingdom of Heaven may be compared to a king
who decided to settle his accounts with his servants. When
the reckoning began, they brought him a man who owed ten
thousand talents; he had no means of paying, so his master gave
orders that he should be sold, together with his wife and children
and all his possessions, to meet the debt. At this, the servant
threw himself down at his master's feet, with the words, 'Be
patient with me and I will pay the whole sum.' And the servant's

61

master felt so sorry for him that he let him go and canceled the debt. Now as this servant went out, he happened to meet a fellow-servant who owed him one hundred denarii; and he seized him by the throat and began to throttle him, saying, 'Pay what you owe me.' His fellow-servant fell at his feet and appealed to him, saying, 'Be patient with me and I will pay you.' But the other would not agree; on the contrary, he had him thrown into prison till he should pay the debt. His fellow-servants were deeply distressed when they saw what had happened, and they went to their master and reported the whole affair to him. Then the master sent for the man and said to him, 'You wicked servant, I canceled all that debt of yours when you appealed to me. Were you not bound, then, to have pity on your fellow-servant just as I had pity on you?' And in his anger the master handed him over to

the torturers till he should pay all his debt. And that is how my
heavenly Father will deal with you unless you each forgive your
brother from your heart."

MATTHEW 18:23–35

"WHO IS MY NEIGHBOR?"

"A man was once on his way down from Jerusalem to Jericho and
fell into the hands of bandits; they stripped him, beat him and
then made off, leaving him half dead. Now a priest happened to
be traveling down the same road, but when he saw the man, he
passed by on the other side. In the same way a Levite who came to
the place saw him, and passed by on the other side. But a
Samaritan traveler who came on him was moved with compassion
when he saw him. He went up to him and bandaged his wounds,
pouring oil and wine on them. He then lifted him onto his own
mount and took him to an inn and looked after him. Next day, he

took out two denarii and handed them to the innkeeper and said,
'Look after him, and on my way back I will make good any extra
expense you have.' Which of these three, do you think, proved
himself a neighbor to the man who fell into the bandits' hands?"
He replied, "The one who showed pity toward him." Jesus said to
him, "Go, and do the same yourself."

LUKE 10:30–37

THE BETTER PART

In the course of their journey he came to a village, and a woman
named Martha welcomed him into her house. She had a sister
called Mary, who sat down at the Lord's feet and listened to him
speaking. Now Martha, who was distracted with all the serving,
came to him and said, "Lord, do you not care that my sister is
leaving me to do the serving all by myself? Please tell her to help
me." But the Lord answered, "Martha, Martha," he said, "you

worry and fret about so many things, and yet few are needed, indeed only one. It is Mary who has chosen the better part, and it is not to be taken from her."

LUKE 10:38–42

BE PERSISTENT WITH GOD

"Suppose one of you has a friend and goes to him in the middle of the night to say, 'My friend, lend me three loaves, because a friend of mine on his travels has just arrived at my house and I have nothing to offer him;' and the man answers from inside the house, 'Do not bother me. The door is bolted now, and my children are with me in bed; I cannot get up to give it to you.' I tell you, if the man does not get up and give it him for friendship's sake, persistence will make him get up and give his friend all he wants."

LUKE 11:5–8

GIVE BIRTH TO THE WORD OF GOD

It happened that as he was speaking, a woman in the crowd raised her voice and said, "Blessed the womb that bore you and the breasts that fed you." But he replied, "More blessed still are those who hear the word of God and keep it!"

LUKE 11:27–28

JESUS' WARNINGS

THE FOOLISH RICH MAN

A man in the crowd said to him, "Master, tell my brother to give me a share of our inheritance." He said to him, "My friend, who appointed me your judge, or the arbitrator of your claims?" Then he said to them, "Watch, and be on your guard against avarice of any kind, for life does not consist in possessions, even when someone has more than he needs."

Then he told them a parable, "There was once a rich man who, having had a good harvest from his land, thought to himself, 'What am I to do? I have not enough room to store my crops.' Then he said, 'This is what I will do: I will pull down my barns and build bigger ones, and store all my grain and my goods in them, and I will say to my soul: My soul, you have plenty of good things laid by for many years to come; take things easy, eat, drink, have a good time.' But God said to him, 'Fool! This very night the demand will be made for your soul; and this hoard of yours, whose will it be then?' So it is when someone stores up treasure for himself instead of becoming rich in the sight of God."

LUKE 12:13–21

GOD WILL NOT WAIT FOREVER

Some people arrived and told him about the Galileans whose blood Pilate had mingled with that of their sacrifices. At this he said to them, "Do you suppose that these Galileans were worse sinners than any others, that this should have happened to them? They were not, I tell you. No; but unless you repent you will all perish as they did. Or those eighteen on whom the tower at Siloam fell, killing them all? Do you suppose that they were more guilty than all the other people living in Jerusalem? They were not, I tell you. No; but unless you repent you will all perish as they did."

He told this parable, "A man had a fig tree planted in his vineyard, and he came looking for fruit on it but found none. He said to his vinedresser, 'For three years now I have been coming to look for fruit on this fig tree and finding none. Cut it down: why should it be taking up the ground?' 'Sir,' the man replied, 'leave it one more year and give me time to dig round it and manure it: it may bear fruit next year; if not, then you can cut it down.'"

LUKE 13:1–9

One Sabbath day he was teaching in one of the synagogues, and there before him was a woman who for eighteen years had been possessed by a spirit that crippled her; she was bent double and quite unable to stand upright. When Jesus saw her he called her over and said, "Woman, you are freed from your disability," and he laid his hands on her. And at once she straightened up, and she glorified God.

But the president of the synagogue was indignant because Jesus had healed on the Sabbath, and he addressed all those present saying, "There are six days when work is to be done. Come and be healed on one of those days and not on the Sabbath." But the Lord answered him and said, "Hypocrites! Is there one of you who does not untie his ox or his donkey from the manger on the Sabbath and take it out for watering? And this woman, a daughter of Abraham whom Satan has held bound these eighteen years—was it not right to untie this bond on the

Sabbath day?" When he said this, all his adversaries were covered
with confusion, and all the people were overjoyed at all the
wonders he worked.

LUKE 13:10–17

JESUS WEEPS OVER JERUSALEM

"Jerusalem, Jerusalem, you that kill the prophets and stone
those who are sent to you! How often have I longed to gather
your children together, as a hen gathers her brood under her
wings, and you refused! Look! Your house will be left to you.
Yes, I promise you, you shall not see me till the time comes
when you are saying:

Blessed is he who is coming in the name of the Lord!"

LUKE 13:34–35

HOW TO THROW A PARTY

"When you give a lunch or a dinner, do not invite your friends or
your brothers or your relations or rich neighbors, in case they
invite you back and so repay you. No; when you have a party,
invite the poor, the crippled, the lame, the blind; then you will
be blessed, for they have no means to repay you and so you will be
repaid when the upright rise again."

LUKE 14:12–14

HOW TO BEHAVE AT A PARTY

"When someone invites you to a wedding feast, do not take your
seat in the place of honor. A more distinguished person than you
may have been invited, and the person who invited you both may
come and say, 'Give up your place to this man.' And then, to your
embarrassment, you will have to go and take the lowest place.

No; when you are a guest, make your way to the lowest place and sit there, so that, when your host comes, he may say, 'My friend, move up higher.' Then, everyone with you at the table will see you honored. For everyone who raises himself up will be humbled, and the one who humbles himself will be raised up."

LUKE 14:8–11

THE LOST COIN

"Or again, what woman with ten drachmas would not, if she lost one, light a lamp and sweep out the house and search thoroughly till she found it? And then, when she had found it, call together her friends and neighbors, saying to them, 'Rejoice with me, I have found the drachma I lost.' In the same way, I tell you, there is rejoicing among the angels of God over one repentant sinner."

LUKE 15:8–10

"There was a man who had two sons. The younger one said to his father, 'Father, let me have the share of the estate that will come to me.' So the father divided the property between them. A few days later, the younger son got together everything he had and left for a distant country where he squandered his money on a life of debauchery.

"When he had spent it all, that country experienced a severe famine, and now he began to feel the pinch so he hired himself out to one of the local inhabitants who put him on his farm to feed the pigs. And he would willingly have filled himself with the husks the pigs were eating but no one would let him have them. Then he came to his senses and said, 'How many of my father's hired men have all the food they want and more, and here am I dying of hunger! I will leave this place and go to my father and say: Father, I have sinned against heaven and against you; I no longer deserve to be called your son; treat me as one of your hired men.' So he left the place and went back to his father.

"While he was still a long way off, his father saw him and was moved with pity. He ran to the boy, clasped him in his arms and kissed him. Then his son said, 'Father, I have sinned against heaven and against you. I no longer deserve to be called your son.' But the father said to his servants, 'Quick! Bring out the best robe and put it on him; put a ring on his finger and sandals on his feet. Bring the calf we have been fattening, and kill it; we will celebrate by having a feast, because this son of mine was dead and has come back to life; he was lost and is found.' And they began to celebrate."

LUKE 15:11–24

THE PRODIGAL SON'S OLDER BROTHER

"Now the elder son was out in the fields, and on his way back, as he drew near the house, he could hear music and dancing. Calling one of the servants he asked what it was all about. The servant told him, 'Your brother has come, and your father has killed the calf we had been fattening because he has got him back safe and sound.' He was angry then and refused to go in, and his father came out and began to urge him to come in; but he retorted to his father, 'All these years I have slaved for you and never once disobeyed any orders of yours, yet you never offered me so much as a kid for me to celebrate with my friends. But, for this son of yours, when he comes back after swallowing up your property—he and his loose women—you kill the calf we had been fattening.'

"The father said, 'My son, you are with me always and all I have is yours. But it was only right we should celebrate and rejoice, because your brother here was dead and has come to life; he was lost and is found.' "

LUKE 15:25–32

THE BEGGAR'S REWARD

"There was a rich man who used to dress in purple and fine linen and feast magnificently every day. And at his gate there used to lie a poor man called Lazarus, covered with sores, who longed to fill himself with what fell from the rich man's table. Even dogs came and licked his sores. Now it happened that the poor man died and was carried away by the angels into Abraham's embrace. The rich man also died and was buried.

"In his torment in Hades he looked up and saw Abraham a long way off with Lazarus in his embrace. So he cried out, 'Father Abraham, pity me and send Lazarus to dip the tip of his finger in water and cool my tongue, for I am in agony in these flames.' Abraham said, 'My son, remember that during your life you had your fill of good things, just as Lazarus his fill of bad. Now he is being comforted here while you are in agony. But that is not all: between us and you a great gulf has been fixed, to prevent those who want to cross from our side to yours or from your side to ours.'

"So he said, 'Father, I beg you then to send Lazarus to my father's house, since I have five brothers, to give them warning so that they do not come to this place of torment too.' Abraham said, 'They have Moses and the prophets, let them listen to them.' The rich man replied, 'Ah no, father Abraham, but if someone comes to them from the dead, they will repent.' Then Abraham said to him, 'If they will not listen either to Moses or to the prophets, they will not be convinced even if someone should rise from the dead.' "

LUKE 16:19–31

Abraham is the father of the Jewish people. Those who lived good lives were said to go to "Abraham's bosom" when they died.

DO NOT LOOK FOR THANKS

"Which of you, with a servant plowing or minding sheep, would say to him when he returned from the fields, 'Come and have your meal at once'? Would he not be more likely to say, 'Get my supper ready; fasten your belt and wait on me while I eat and drink. You yourself can eat and drink afterward'? Must he be grateful to the servant for doing what he was told? So with you: when you have done all you have been told to do, say, 'We are useless servants: we have done no more than our duty.' "

LUKE 17:7–10

BUT REMEMBER TO SAY THANKS

Now it happened that on the way to Jerusalem he was traveling in the borderlands of Samaria and Galilee. As he entered one of the villages, ten men suffering from a virulent skin-disease came to meet him. They stood some way off and called to him, "Jesus! Master! Take pity on us." When he saw them he said, "Go and show yourselves to the priests." Now as they were going away they were cleansed. Finding himself cured, one of them turned back praising God at the top of his voice and threw himself prostrate at the feet of Jesus and thanked him. The man was a Samaritan. This led Jesus to say, "Were not all ten made clean? The other nine, where are they? It seems that no one has come back to give praise to God, except this foreigner." And he said to the man, "Stand up and go on your way. Your faith has saved you."

LUKE 17:11–19

THE QUIET KINGDOM

Asked by the Pharisees when the kingdom of God was to come, he gave them this answer, "The coming of the kingdom of God does not admit of observation and there will be no one to say, 'Look, it is here! Look, it is there!' For look, the kingdom of God is among you."

LUKE 17:20–21

THE TIME OF GOD'S JUSTICE

Then he told them a parable about the need to pray continually and never lose heart. "There was a judge in a certain town," he said, "who had neither fear of God nor respect for anyone. In the same town there was also a widow who kept on coming to him and saying, 'I want justice from you against my enemy!' For a long time he refused, but at last he said to himself, 'Even though

I have neither fear of God nor respect for any human person, I must give this widow her just rights since she keeps pestering me, or she will come and slap me in the face.'

"You notice what the unjust judge has to say? Now, will not God see justice done to his elect if they keep calling to him day and night even though he still delays to help them? I promise you, he will see justice done to them, and done speedily. But when the Son of man comes, will he find any faith on earth?"

LUKE 18:1–8

THE PHARISEE AND THE PUBLICAN

"Two men went up to the Temple to pray, one a Pharisee, the other a tax collector. The Pharisee stood there and said this prayer to himself, 'I thank you, God, that I am not grasping, unjust, adulterous like everyone else, and particularly that I am not like this tax collector here. I fast twice a week; I pay tithes on all I get.' The tax collector stood some distance away, not daring even to raise his eyes to heaven; but he beat his breast and said, 'God, be merciful to me, a sinner.' This man, I tell you, went home again justified; the other did not. For everyone who raises himself up will be humbled, but anyone who humbles himself will be raised up."

LUKE 18:10–14

Publican, the old word for tax collector, is the name by which this character is traditionally known. The Roman tax collectors were universally hated, even though theirs was an unenviable lot: they had to make up everyone else's defaults out of their own pockets!

WHO OWNS GOD'S KINGDOM?

"Let the little children alone, and do not stop them from coming to me; for it is to such as these that the kingdom of Heaven belongs." Then he laid his hands on them and went on his way.

MATTHEW 19:14–15

THE HANDICAP OF WEALTH

And now a man came to him and asked, "Master, what good deed must I do to possess eternal life?" Jesus said to him, "Why do you ask me about what is good? There is one alone who is good. But if you wish to enter into life, keep the commandments." He said, "Which ones?" Jesus replied, "These: *You shall not kill. You shall not commit adultery. You shall not steal. You shall not give false witness. Honor your father and your mother. You shall love your neighbor as yourself."* The young man said to him, "I have kept all these. What more do I need to do?" Jesus said, "If you wish to be perfect, go and sell your possessions and give the money to the poor, and you will have treasure in heaven; then come, follow me." But when the young man heard these words he went away sad, for he was a man of great wealth.

Then Jesus said to his disciples, "In truth I tell you, it is hard for someone rich to enter the kingdom of Heaven. Yes, I tell you again, it is easier for a camel to pass through the eye of a needle than for someone rich to enter the kingdom of Heaven."

When the disciples heard this they were astonished. "Who can be saved then?" they said. Jesus gazed at them. "By human resources," he told them, "this is impossible; for God everything is possible."

MATTHEW 19:16–26

"Now the kingdom of Heaven is like a landowner going out at daybreak to hire workers for his vineyard. He made an agreement with the workers for one denarius a day and sent them to his vineyard. Going out at about the third hour he saw others standing idle in the market place and said to them, 'You go to my vineyard too and I will give you a fair wage.' So they went. At about the sixth hour and again at about the ninth hour, he went out and did the same. Then at about the eleventh hour he went out and found more men standing around, and he said to them, 'Why have you been standing here idle all day?' 'Because no one has hired us,' they answered. He said to them, 'You go into my vineyard too.' In the evening, the owner of the vineyard said to his bailiff, 'Call the workers and pay them their wages, starting with the last arrivals and ending with the first.'

So those who were hired at about the eleventh hour came forward and received one denarius each. When the first came, they expected to get more, but they too received one denarius each. They took it, but grumbled at the landowner saying, 'The men who came last have done only one hour, and you have treated them the same as us, though we have done a heavy day's work in all the heat.' He answered one of them and said, 'My friend, I am not being unjust to you; did we not agree on one denarius? Take your earnings and go. I choose to pay the lastcomer as much as I pay you. Have I no right to do what I like with my own? Why should you be envious because I am generous?' Thus the last will be first, and the first, last."

MATTHEW 20:1–16

THE GATHERING STORM

ON THE ROAD TO JERUSALEM,
JESUS PREDICTS HIS FATE FOR THE THIRD TIME

They were on the road, going up to Jerusalem; Jesus was walking on ahead of them; they were in a daze, and those who followed were apprehensive. Once more taking the Twelve aside he began to tell them what was going to happen to him, "Now we are going up to Jerusalem, and the Son of man is about to be handed over to the chief priests and the scribes. They will condemn him to death and will hand him over to the gentiles, who will mock

him and spit at him and scourge him and put him to death; and
after three days he will rise again."

MARK 10:32–34

MRS. ZEBEDEE PUSHES HER SONS FORWARD

Then the mother of Zebedee's sons came with her sons to make a
request of him, and bowed low; and he said to her, "What is it
you want?" She said to him, "Promise that these two sons of mine
may sit one at your right hand and the other at your left in your
kingdom." Jesus answered, "You do not know what you are
asking. Can you drink the cup that I am going to drink?" They
replied, "We can." He said to them, "Very well; you shall drink
my cup, but as for seats at my right hand and my left, these are
not mine to grant; they belong to those to whom they have been
allotted by my Father."

MATTHEW 20:20–23

WHO'S IN CHARGE HERE, ANYWAY?

When the other ten heard this they were indignant with the two brothers. But Jesus called them to him and said, "You know that among the gentiles the rulers lord it over them, and great men make their authority felt. Among you this is not to happen. No; anyone who wants to become great among you must be your servant, and anyone who wants to be first among you must be your slave, just as the Son of man came not to be served but to serve, and to give his life as a ransom for many."

MATTHEW 20:24–28

BLIND BARTIMAEUS PERSISTS

They reached Jericho; and as he left Jericho with his disciples and a great crowd, Bartimaeus—that is, the son of Timaeus—a blind beggar, was sitting at the side of the road. When he heard that it was Jesus of Nazareth, he began to shout and cry out. "Son of David, Jesus, have pity on me." And many of them scolded him and told him to keep quiet, but he only shouted all the louder, "Son of David, have pity on me." Jesus stopped and said, "Call him here." So they called the blind man over. "Courage," they said, "get up; he is calling you." So throwing off his cloak, he jumped up and went to Jesus. Then Jesus spoke, "What do you want me to do for you?" The blind man said to him, "Rabbuni, let me see again." Jesus said to him, "Go; your faith has saved you." And at once his sight returned and he followed him along the road.

MARK 10:46–52

ZACCHAEUS, THE LITTLE SINNER

He entered Jericho and was going through the town and suddenly a man whose name was Zacchaeus made his appearance;

he was one of the senior tax collectors and a wealthy man. He
kept trying to see which Jesus was, but he was too short and
could not see him for the crowd; so he ran ahead and climbed a
sycamore tree to catch a glimpse of Jesus who was to pass that
way. When Jesus reached the spot he looked up and spoke to him.
"Zacchaeus, come down. Hurry, because I am to stay at your
house today." And he hurried down and welcomed him joyfully.
They all complained when they saw what was happening. "He has
gone to stay at a sinner's house," they said. But Zacchaeus stood
his ground and said to the Lord, "Look, sir, I am going to give
half my property to the poor, and if I have cheated anybody I will
pay him back four times the amount." And Jesus said to him,
"Today salvation has come to this house, because this man too is a
son of Abraham; for the Son of man has come to seek out and save
what was lost."

LUKE 19:1–10

JESUS CREATES HAVOC

And when he entered Jerusalem, the whole city was in turmoil as people asked, "Who is this?" and the crowds answered, "This is the prophet Jesus from Nazareth in Galilee."

Jesus then went into the Temple and drove out all those who were selling and buying there; he upset the tables of the money-changers and the seats of the dove-sellers. He said to them, "According to scripture, *my house will be called a house of prayer;* but you are turning it into a *bandits' den.*" There were also blind and lame people who came to him in the Temple, and he cured them. At the sight of the wonderful things he did and of the children shouting, "Hosanna to the son of David" in the Temple, the chief priests and the scribes were indignant and said to him, "Do you hear what they are saying?" Jesus answered,

"Yes. Have you never read this:

> *By the mouths of children, babes in arms,*
> *you have made sure of praise?"*

MATTHEW 21:10–16

"Son of David" was a name of the Messiah, which, applied to Jesus by the children, scandalized the religious authorities.

JESUS THROWS A CURVE BALL

He had gone into the Temple and was teaching, when the chief priests and the elders of the people came to him and said, "What authority have you for acting like this? And who gave you this authority?" In reply Jesus said to them, "And I will ask you a question, just one; if you tell me the answer to it, then I will tell you my authority for acting like this. John's baptism, what was its origin, heavenly or human?" And they argued this way among themselves, "If we say heavenly, he will retort to us, 'Then why did you refuse to believe him?'; but if we say human, we have the people to fear, for they all hold that John was a prophet." So their reply to Jesus was, "We do not know." And he retorted to them, "Nor will I tell you my authority for acting like this."

MATTHEW 21:23–27

WHOM WILL GOD WELCOME?

"What is your opinion? A man had two sons. He went and said to the first, 'My boy, go and work in the vineyard today.' He answered, 'I will not go,' but afterward thought better of it and went. The man then went and said the same thing to the second who answered, 'Certainly, sir,' but did not go. Which of the two did the father's will?" They said, "The first." Jesus said to them,

"In truth I tell you, tax collectors and prostitutes are making their way into the kingdom of God before you."

MATTHEW 21:28–31

JESUS GETS PRETTY EXPLICIT . . .

"Listen to another parable. There was a man, a landowner, who planted a vineyard; he fenced it round, dug a winepress in it and built a tower; then he leased it to tenants and went abroad. When vintage time drew near he sent his servants to the tenants to collect his produce. But the tenants seized his servants, thrashed one, killed another and stoned a third. Next he sent some more servants, this time a larger number, and they dealt with them in the same way. Finally he sent his son to them thinking, 'They will respect my son.' But when the tenants saw the son, they said to each other, 'This is the heir. Come on, let us kill him and take over his inheritance.' So they seized him and threw him out of the vineyard and killed him. Now when the owner of the vineyard comes, what will he do to those tenants?" They answered, "He will bring those wretches to a wretched end and lease the vineyard to other tenants who will deliver the produce to him at the proper time." Jesus said to them, "Have you never read in the scriptures:

The stone which the builders rejected
has become the cornerstone;
this is the Lord's doing
and we marvel at it?

"I tell you, then, that the kingdom of God will be taken from you and given to a people who will produce its fruit."

MATTHEW 21:33–43

When they heard his parables, the chief priests and the scribes realized he was speaking about them, but though they would have liked to arrest him they were afraid of the crowds, who looked on him as a prophet.

MATTHEW 21:45–46

WHAT HAPPENS WHEN WE REFUSE GOD'S INVITATION

"The kingdom of Heaven may be compared to a king who gave a feast for his son's wedding. He sent his servants to call those who had been invited, but they would not come. Next he sent some more servants with the words, 'Tell those who have been invited: Look, my banquet is all prepared, my oxen and fattened cattle have been slaughtered, everything is ready. Come to the wedding.' But they were not interested: one went off to his farm, another to his business, and the rest seized his servants, maltreated them and killed them. The king was furious. He despatched his troops, destroyed those murderers and burnt their town. Then he said to his servants, 'The wedding is ready; but as those who were invited proved to be unworthy, go to the main crossroads and invite everyone you can find to come to the wedding.' . . . For many are invited but not all are chosen."

MATTHEW 22:2–10; 14

FAITH WITHOUT ACTION

"So these servants went out onto the roads and collected together everyone they could find, bad and good alike; and the wedding hall was filled with guests. When the king came in to look at the guests he noticed one man who was not wearing a wedding garment, and said to him, 'How did you get in here, my friend, without a wedding garment?' And the man was silent. Then the king said to the attendants, 'Bind him hand and foot and throw him into the darkness outside, where there will be weeping and grinding of teeth.' "

MATTHEW 22:10–13

THE PHARISEES SET A TRAP

Next they sent to him some Pharisees and some Herodians to catch him out in what he said. These came and said to him, "Master, we know that you are an honest man, that you are not afraid of anyone, because human rank means nothing to you, and that you teach the way of God in all honesty. Is it permissible to pay taxes to Caesar or not? Should we pay or not?" Recognizing their hypocrisy he said to them, "Why are you putting me to the test? Hand me a denarius and let me see it." They handed him one and he said to them, "Whose portrait is this? Whose title?"

They said to him, "Caesar's." Jesus said to them, "Pay Caesar what belongs to Caesar—and God what belongs to God." And they were amazed at him.

MARK 12:13–17

JESUS QUOTES THE TORAH

One of the scribes who had listened to them debating appreciated that Jesus had given a good answer and put a further question to him, "Which is the first of all the commandments?" Jesus replied, "This is the first: *Listen, Israel, the Lord our God is the one, only Lord, and you must love the Lord your God with all your heart, with all your soul,* with all your mind *and with all your strength.* The second is this: *You must love your neighbor as yourself.* There is no commandment greater than these."

MARK 12:28–31

Many Christians wrongly assume that Jesus' Law of Love—for God and neighbor— represents a kind of evolutionary improvement on the (supposedly) more calculating laws of the Old Testament. But though Jesus may be prioritizing these laws, he is also quoting from the Great Law (or Torah) of the Jews, as contained in the first five books of the Bible. The first commandment enunciated by Jesus is a word-for-word quotation from Judaism's most sacred text, the Sh'ma, as found in Deuteronomy 6:4–5. The second commandment—to love one's neighbor as oneself—was first set down in Leviticus 19:18.

ANOTHER CURVE BALL

> While the Pharisees were gathered round, Jesus put to them this question, "What is your opinion about the Christ? Whose son is he?" They told him, "David's." He said to them, "Then how is it that David, moved by the Spirit, calls him Lord, where he says:

The Lord declared to my Lord,
take your seat at my right hand,
till I have made your enemies
your footstool?

If David calls him Lord, how then can he be his son?" No one could think of anything to say in reply, and from that day no one dared to ask him any further questions.

MATTHEW 22:41–46

JESUS ATTACKS THE CHURCH HEAD-ON

Then addressing the crowds and his disciples Jesus said, "The scribes and the Pharisees occupy the chair of Moses. You must therefore do and observe what they tell you; but do not be guided by what they do, since they do not practice what they preach."

MATTHEW 23:1–3

This entire chapter (Matthew 23) is a scathing attack on the religious establish-ment of first-century Palestine. To occupy someone's chair meant in ancient times to speak with his authority. So "the scribes and Pharisees" are to be obeyed because they speak with the authority of Moses, the greatest of all Jewish prophets, but they are not to be imitated—because they are frauds. To limit Jesus' criticism to the religious establishment of his own day, however, would be to miss its universal and timeless message. The words "church" and "synagogue" mean the same thing: meeting or assembly. No churchman or churchwoman of our day—indeed, no fig-ure of religious authority—can afford to pretend that Jesus' words are not addressed to him or her.

THE CHURCH DEVISES NOVEL OBLIGATIONS, THEN SHUNS ITS OWN RESPONSIBILITIES

They tie up heavy burdens and lay them on people's shoulders,
but will they lift a finger to move them? Not they!

MATTHEW 23:4

CHURCHMEN LOVE THE LIMELIGHT

"Everything they do is done to attract attention, like wearing broader headbands and longer tassels, like wanting to take the place of honor at banquets and the front seats in the synagogues, being greeted respectfully in the market squares and having people call them Rabbi."

MATTHEW 23:5–7

TRUE DISCIPLES SHUN TITLES AND SPECIAL TREATMENT

"You, however, must not allow yourselves to be called Rabbi, since you have only one Master, and you are all brothers. You must call no one on earth your father, since you have only one Father, and he is in heaven. Nor must you allow yourselves to be

105

called teachers, for you have only one Teacher, the Christ. The greatest among you must be your servant. Anyone who raises himself up will be humbled, and anyone who humbles himself will be raised up."

MATTHEW 23:8–12

THE CHURCH DENIES PEOPLE ACCESS TO GOD

"Alas for you, scribes and Pharisees, you hypocrites! You shut up the kingdom of Heaven in people's faces, neither going in yourselves nor allowing others to go in who want to."

MATTHEW 23:13

THE CHURCH CORRUPTS EVEN SINCERE SEEKERS

"Alas for you, scribes and Pharisees, you hypocrites! You travel over sea and land to make a single proselyte, and anyone who becomes one you make twice as fit for hell as you are."

MATTHEW 23:15

CHURCHMEN MAKE HYPOCRITICAL DISTINCTIONS

"Alas for you, blind guides! You say, 'If anyone swears by the Temple, it has no force; but anyone who swears by the gold of the Temple is bound.' Fools and blind! For which is of greater value, the gold or the Temple that makes the gold sacred? Again, 'If anyone swears by the altar it has no force; but anyone who swears by the offering on the altar, is bound.' You blind men! For which is of greater worth, the offering or the altar that makes the offering sacred? Therefore, someone who

107

swears by the altar is swearing by that and by everything on it.
And someone who swears by the Temple is swearing by that
and by the One who dwells in it. And someone who swears by
heaven is swearing by the throne of God and by the One who
is seated there."

MATTHEW 23:16–22

THE CHURCH'S PRIORITIES ARE UPSIDE DOWN

"Alas for you, scribes and Pharisees, you hypocrites! You pay your
tithe of mint and dill and cummin and have neglected the
weightier matters of the Law—justice, mercy, good faith! These
you should have practiced, those not neglected. You blind guides,
straining out gnats and swallowing camels!"

MATTHEW 23:23–24

CHURCHMEN VALUE APPEARANCES ABOVE ALL ELSE

"Alas for you, scribes and Pharisees, you hypocrites! You clean the outside of cup and dish and leave the inside full of extortion and intemperance. Blind Pharisee! Clean the inside of cup and dish first so that it and the outside are both clean.

"Alas for you, scribes and Pharisees, you hypocrites! You are like whitewashed tombs that look handsome on the outside, but inside are full of the bones of the dead and every kind of corruption. In just the same way, from the outside you look upright, but inside you are full of hypocrisy and lawlessness."

MATTHEW 23:25–28

JESUS WILL RETURN LIKE A THIEF IN THE NIGHT

"As it was in Noah's day, so will it be when the Son of man comes. For in those days before the Flood people were eating,

drinking, taking wives, taking husbands, right up to the day
Noah went into the ark, and they suspected nothing till the
Flood came and swept them all away. This is what it will be like
when the Son of man comes. Then of two men in the fields, one is
taken, one left; of two women grinding at the mill, one is taken,
one left.

"So stay awake, because you do not know the day when your
master is coming. You may be quite sure of this, that if the
householder had known at what time of the night the burglar
would come, he would have stayed awake and would not have
allowed anyone to break through the wall of his house. Therefore,
you too must stand ready because the Son of man is coming at an
hour you do not expect."

MATTHEW 24:37–44

BE A CONSCIENTIOUS STEWARD
OF WHATEVER GOD HAS PLACED IN YOUR CARE

"Who, then, is the wise and trustworthy servant whom the master placed over his household to give them their food at the proper time? Blessed that servant if his master's arrival finds him doing exactly that. In truth I tell you, he will put him in charge of everything he owns. But if the servant is dishonest and says to himself, 'My master is taking his time,' and sets about beating his fellow-servants and eating and drinking with drunkards, his master will come on a day he does not expect and at an hour he does not know. The master will cut him off and send him to the same fate as the hypocrites, where there will be weeping and grinding of teeth."

MATTHEW 24:45–51

"Then the kingdom of Heaven will be like this: Ten wedding attendants took their lamps and went to meet the bridegroom. Five of them were foolish and five were sensible: the foolish ones, though they took their lamps, took no oil with them, whereas the sensible ones took flasks of oil as well as their lamps. The bridegroom was late, and they all grew drowsy and fell asleep. But at midnight there was a cry. 'Look! The bridegroom! Go out and meet him.' Then all those wedding attendants woke up and trimmed their lamps, and the foolish ones said to the sensible ones, 'Give us some of your oil: our lamps are going out.' But they replied, 'There may not be enough for us and for you; you had better go to those who sell it and buy some for yourselves.' They had gone off to buy it when the bridegroom arrived. Those who were ready went in with him to the wedding hall and the door was closed. The other attendants arrived later. 'Lord, Lord,' they said, 'open the door for us.' But he replied, 'In truth I tell you, I do not know you.' So stay awake, because you do not know either the day or the hour."

MATTHEW 25:1–13

In the older translations, these wise and foolish wedding attendants were called "virgins," which meant no more than that they were young, unmarried women.

INVEST YOUR TALENTS . . .

"It is like a man about to go abroad who summoned his servants and entrusted his property to them. To one he gave five talents, to another two, to a third one, each in proportion to his ability. Then he set out on his journey. The man who had received the five talents promptly went and traded with them and made five more. The man who had received two made two more in the same way. But the man who had received one went off and dug a hole in the ground and hid his master's money. Now a long time afterward, the master of those servants came back and went through his accounts with them. The man who had received the five talents came forward bringing five more. 'Sir,' he said, 'you entrusted me with five talents; here are five more that I have made.' His master said to him, 'Well done, good and trustworthy servant; you have shown you are trustworthy in small things; I will trust you with greater; come and join in your master's happiness.' Next the man with the two talents came forward. 'Sir,' he said, 'you entrusted me with two talents; here are two more that I have made.' His master said to him, 'Well done, good and trustworthy servant; you have shown you are trustworthy in small things; I will trust you with greater; come and join in your master's happiness.' "

MATTHEW 25:14–22

. . . OR ELSE!

"Last came forward the man who had the single talent. 'Sir,' said he, 'I had heard you were a hard man, reaping where you had not sown and gathering where you had not scattered; so I was afraid, and I went off and hid your talent in the ground. Here it is; it was yours, you have it back.' But his master answered him, 'You wicked and lazy servant! So you knew that I reap where I have not sown and gather where I have not scattered? Well then, you should have deposited my money with the bankers, and on my return I would have got my money back with interest. So now, take the talent from him and give it to the man who has the ten talents. For to everyone who has will be given more, and he will have more than enough; but anyone who has not, will be deprived even of what he has. As for this good-for-nothing servant, throw him into the darkness outside, where there will be weeping and grinding of teeth.' "

MATTHEW 25:24–30   **115**

"When the Son of man comes in his glory, escorted by all the
angels, then he will take his seat on his throne of glory. All
nations will be assembled before him and he will separate people
one from another as the shepherd separates sheep from goats. He
will place the sheep on his right hand and the goats on his left.
Then the King will say to those on his right hand, 'Come, you
whom my Father has blessed, take as your heritage the kingdom
prepared for you since the foundation of the world. For I was
hungry and you gave me food, I was thirsty and you gave me
drink, I was a stranger and you made me welcome, lacking
clothes and you clothed me, sick and you visited me, in prison
and you came to see me.' Then the upright will say to him in
reply, 'Lord, when did we see you hungry and feed you, or thirsty
and give you drink? When did we see you a stranger and make
you welcome, lacking clothes and clothe you? When did we find
you sick or in prison and go to see you?' And the King will

answer, 'In truth I tell you, in so far as you did this to one of the least of these brothers of mine, you did it to me.' "

MATTHEW 25:31–40

. . . AND SEND THE UNJUST AWAY

"Then he will say to those on his left hand, 'Go away from me, with your curse upon you, to the eternal fire prepared for the devil and his angels. For I was hungry and you never gave me food, I was thirsty and you never gave me anything to drink, I was a stranger and you never made me welcome, lacking clothes and you never clothed me, sick and in prison and you never visited me.' Then it will be their turn to ask, 'Lord, when did we see you hungry or thirsty, a stranger or lacking clothes, sick or in prison, and did not come to your help?' Then he will answer, 'In truth I tell you, in so far as you neglected to do this to one of the least of these, you neglected to do it to me.' And they will go away to eternal punishment, and the upright to eternal life."

MATTHEW 25:41–46

JESUS COMPLETES HIS TEACHING

Jesus had now finished all he wanted to say, and he told his disciples, "It will be Passover, as you know, in two days' time, and the Son of man will be handed over to be crucified."

MATTHEW 26:1–2

Passover is the feast of the Jews that commemorates their great liberation from slavery in Egypt. The word "passover" refers to the angel of death who (in Exodus 12) "passed over" the houses of the Jewish slaves because these were marked with the blood of a sacrificed lamb. It also refers to the "passing over" of the Chosen People from slavery in Egypt to freedom in the Promised Land. In Christian interpretation, Jesus is the lamb whose blood saves us from death and enables us to pass from the slavery of sin to the freedom of the Kingdom.

JESUS IS ANOINTED

Jesus was at Bethany in the house of Simon, a man who had suffered from a virulent skin-disease, when a woman came to him with an alabaster jar of very expensive ointment, and poured it on his head as he was at table. When they saw this, the disciples said indignantly, "Why this waste? This could have been sold for a high price and the money given the poor." But Jesus noticed this and said, "Why are you upsetting the woman? What she has done for me is indeed a good work! You have the poor with you always, but you will not always have me. When she poured this ointment

on my body, she did it to prepare me for burial. In truth I tell
you, wherever in all the world this gospel is proclaimed, what she
has done will be told as well, in remembrance of her."

MATTHEW 26:6–13

*In this episode, Matthew may mean to show that Jesus, on completing his teaching
and just prior to his suffering and death, was anointed as Messiah (which means
"the Anointed One")—a Messiah whose messianic act will be to die for all. In view
of current contentions about the lack of biblical warrant for women clergy, it is illu-
minating to note that the Anointer, who by performing this high-priestly act may
stand in for God the Father, is a woman.*

THE EMPTYING

THE NEW COVENANT IN JESUS' BLOOD

And he said to them, "I have ardently longed to eat this Passover with you before I suffer; because, I tell you, I shall not eat it until it is fulfilled in the kingdom of God."

Then, taking a cup, he gave thanks and said, "Take this and share it among you, because from now on, I tell you, I shall never again drink wine until the kingdom of God comes."

Then he took bread, and when he had given thanks, he broke it and gave it to them, saying, "This is my body given for you; do this in remembrance of me." He did the same with the cup after supper, and said, "This cup is the new covenant in my blood poured out for you."

LUKE 22:15–20

A covenant is a testament, pact, or solemn agreement, having the same sort of permanent binding power as the one God made with the Jewish people, as told in the pages of their sacred scriptures, which Christians call the Old Testament.

JESUS' PRAYER WILL PREVAIL AGAINST SATAN

"Simon, Simon! Look, Satan has got his wish to sift you all like wheat; but I have prayed for you, Simon, that your faith may not fail, and once you have recovered, you in your turn must strengthen your brothers." "Lord," he answered, "I would be ready to go to prison with you, and to death." Jesus replied, "I tell you, Peter, by the time the cock crows today you will have denied three times that you know me."

LUKE 22:31–34

THE AGONY IN THE GARDEN

Then Jesus came with them to a plot of land called Gethsemane; and he said to his disciples, "Stay here while I go over there to pray." He took Peter and the two sons of Zebedee with him. And he began to feel sadness and anguish.

Then he said to them, "My soul is sorrowful to the point of death. Wait here and stay awake with me." And going on a little further he fell on his face and prayed. "My Father," he said, "if it is possible, let this cup pass me by. Nevertheless, let it be as you, not I, would have it."

MATTHEW 26:36–39 **123**

FLESH AGAINST SPIRIT

He came back to the disciples and found them sleeping, and he said to Peter, "So you had not the strength to stay awake with me for one hour? Stay awake, and pray not to be put to the test. The spirit is willing enough, but human nature is weak." Again, a second time, he went away and prayed: "My Father," he said, "if this cup cannot pass by, but I must drink it, your will be done!" And he came back again and found them sleeping, their eyes were so heavy.

Leaving them there, he went away again and prayed for the third time, repeating the same words. Then he came back to the disciples and said to them, "You can sleep on now and have your rest. Look, the hour has come when the Son of man is to be betrayed into the hands of sinners. Get up! Let us go! Look, my betrayer is not far away."

MATTHEW 26:40–46

THE KISS

Suddenly, while he was still speaking, a number of men appeared, and at the head of them the man called Judas, one of the Twelve, who went up to Jesus to kiss him. Jesus said, "Judas, are you betraying the Son of man with a kiss?" His followers, seeing what was about to happen, said, "Lord, shall we use our swords?" And one of them struck the high priest's servant and cut off his right ear. But at this Jesus said, "That is enough." And touching the man's ear he healed him.

Then Jesus said to the chief priests and captains of the Temple guard and elders who had come for him, "Am I a bandit, that you had to set out with swords and clubs? When I

was among you in the Temple day after day you never made a
move to lay hands on me. But this is your hour; this is the reign
of darkness."

LUKE 22:47–53

JESUS BEFORE PILATE

Jesus, then, was brought before the governor, and the governor
put to him this question, "Are you the king of the Jews?" Jesus
replied, "It is you who say it." But when he was accused by the
chief priests and the elders he refused to answer at all. Pilate then
said to him, "Do you not hear how many charges they have made
against you?" But to the governor's amazement, he offered not a
word in answer to any of the charges.

MATTHEW 27:11–14

JESUS BEFORE HEROD

Pilate . . . asked if the man were a Galilean; and finding that he came under Herod's jurisdiction, he passed him over to Herod, who was also in Jerusalem at that time.

Herod was delighted to see Jesus; he had heard about him and had been wanting for a long time to set eyes on him; moreover, he was hoping to see some miracle worked by him. So he questioned him at some length, but without getting any reply. Meanwhile the chief priests and the scribes were there, vigorously pressing their accusations. Then Herod, together with his guards, treated him with contempt and made fun of him; he put a rich cloak on him and sent him back to Pilate. And though Herod and Pilate had been enemies before, they were reconciled that same day.

LUKE 23:6–12

127

JESUS BEFORE PILATE AGAIN

Pilate then summoned the chief priests and the leading men and the people. He said to them, "You brought this man before me as a popular agitator. Now I have gone into the matter myself in your presence and found no grounds in the man for any of the charges you bring against him. Nor has Herod either, since he has sent him back to us. As you can see, the man has done nothing that deserves death, so I shall have him flogged and then let him go." . . . But they kept on shouting at the top of their voices, demanding that he should be crucified. And their shouts kept growing louder.

Pilate then gave his verdict: their demand was to be granted.

LUKE 23:13–17; 23–24

When they reached the place called The Skull, there they crucified him and the two criminals, one on his right, the other on his left. Jesus said, "Father, forgive them; they do not know what they are doing." Then they cast lots to share out his clothing. . . .

One of the criminals hanging there abused him: "Are you not the Christ? Save yourself and us as well." But the other spoke up and rebuked him. "Have you no fear of God at all?" he said. "You got the same sentence as he did, but in our case we deserved it: we are paying for what we did. But this man has done nothing wrong." Then he said, "Jesus, remember me when you come into your kingdom." He answered him, "In truth I tell you, today you will be with me in paradise."

LUKE 23:33–34; 39–43

JESUS PRAYS TO THE END

From the sixth hour there was darkness over all the land until the ninth hour. And about the ninth hour, Jesus cried out in a loud voice, *"Eli, eli, lama sabachthani?"* that is, *"My God, my God, why have you forsaken me?"* When some of those who stood there heard this, they said, "The man is calling on Elijah," and one of them quickly ran to get a sponge which he filled with vinegar and, putting it on a reed, gave it him to drink.

MATTHEW 27:45–48

In his final agony, Jesus prays Psalm 22, a deeply moving and sustaining prayer that begins in despair but ends in confidence of victory. (See pages 228–231 for the complete text.) The despair, however, is real. From the Agony in the Garden to his death, Jesus seems to lose his sense of God's presence. God stops speaking to him. And this feeling of sudden abandonment may have been his greatest suffering.

THE LAST WORD

Jesus cried out in a loud voice saying, "Father, *into your hands I commit my spirit.*" With these words he breathed his last.

LUKE 23:46

THE EXALTATION

THE EMPTY TOMB

When the Sabbath was over, Mary of Magdala, Mary the mother of James, and Salome, bought spices with which to go and anoint him. And very early in the morning on the first day of the week they went to the tomb when the sun had risen.

They had been saying to one another, "Who will roll away the stone for us from the entrance to the tomb?" But when they looked they saw that the stone—which was very big—had already been rolled back. On entering the tomb they saw a young man in a white robe seated on the right-hand side, and they were struck with amazement. But he said to them, "There is no need to be so amazed. You are looking for Jesus of Nazareth, who was crucified: he has risen, he is not here. See, here is the place where they laid him. But you must go and tell his disciples and Peter, 'He is going ahead of you to Galilee; that is where you will see him, just as he told you.' " And the women came out and ran away from the tomb because they were frightened out of their wits; and they said nothing to anyone, for they were afraid.

MARK 16:1–8

THE RISEN JESUS APPEARS TO TWO WOMEN

And suddenly, coming to meet them, was Jesus. "Greetings," he said. And the women came up to him and, clasping his feet, they did him homage. Then Jesus said to them, "Do not be afraid; go and tell my brothers that they must leave for Galilee; there they will see me."

MATTHEW 28:9–10

Now that very same day, two of them were on their way to a village called Emmaus, seven miles from Jerusalem, and they were talking together about all that had happened. And it happened that as they were talking together and discussing it, Jesus himself came up and walked by their side; but their eyes were prevented from recognizing him. He said to them, "What are all these things that you are discussing as you walk along?" They stopped, their faces downcast.

Then one of them, called Cleopas, answered him, "You must be the only person staying in Jerusalem who does not know the things that have been happening there these last few days." He asked, "What things?" They answered, "All about Jesus of Nazareth, who showed himself a prophet powerful in action and speech before God and the whole people; and how our chief priests and our leaders handed him over to be sentenced to death, and had him crucified. Our own hope had been that he would be the one to set Israel free. And this is not all: two whole days have now gone by since it all happened; and some women from our group have astounded us: they went to the tomb in the early morning, and when they could not find the body, they came back to tell us they had seen a vision of angels who declared he was alive. Some of our friends went to the tomb and found everything exactly as the women had reported, but of him they saw nothing."

Then he said to them, "You foolish men! So slow to believe all that the prophets have said! Was it not necessary that the Christ should suffer before entering into his glory?" Then, starting with Moses and going through all the prophets, he explained to them the passages throughout the scriptures that were about himself.

LUKE 24:13–27

When they drew near to the village to which they were going, he made as if to go on; but they pressed him to stay with them saying, "It is nearly evening, and the day is almost over." So he went in to stay with them. Now while he was with them at table, he took the bread and said the blessing; then he broke it and handed it to them. And their eyes were opened and they recognized him; but he had vanished from their sight. Then they said to each other, "Did not our hearts burn within us as he talked to us on the road and explained the scriptures to us?"

They set out that instant and returned to Jerusalem. There they found the Eleven assembled together with their companions, who said to them, "The Lord has indeed risen and has appeared to Simon." Then they told their story of what had happened on the road and how they had recognized him at the breaking of bread.

LUKE 24:28–35

THE RISEN JESUS APPEARS TO ALL

They were still talking about all this when he himself stood among them and said to them, "Peace be with you!" In a state of alarm and fright, they thought they were seeing a ghost. But he said, "Why are you so agitated, and why are these doubts stirring in your hearts? See by my hands and my feet that it is I myself. Touch me and see for yourselves; a ghost has no flesh and bones as you can see I have." And as he said this he showed them his hands and his feet. Their joy was so great that they still could not believe it, as they were dumbfounded; so he said to them, "Have you anything here to eat?" And they offered him a piece of grilled fish, which he took and ate before their eyes.

LUKE 24:36–43

Then he told them, "This is what I meant when I said, while I was still with you, that everything written about me in the Law of Moses, in the Prophets and in the Psalms, was destined to be fulfilled." He then opened their minds to understand the scriptures, and he said to them, "So it is written that the Christ would suffer and on the third day rise from the dead, and that, in his name, repentance for the forgiveness of sins would be preached to all nations, beginning from Jerusalem. You are witnesses to this.

"And now I am sending upon you what the Father has promised. Stay in the city, then, until you are clothed with the power from on high."

LUKE 24:44–49

"The power from on high" is a reference to the descent of God's Spirit upon the disciples, an event described in the second chapter of Luke's second work, The Acts of

the Apostles, which is the only narrative book of the New Testament besides the gospels.

THE LAST BLESSING

Then he took them out as far as the outskirts of Bethany, and raising his hands he blessed them. Now as he blessed them, he withdrew from them and was carried up to heaven. They worshipped him and then went back to Jerusalem full of joy; and they were continually in the Temple praising God.

LUKE 24:50–53

THE PERSONALITIES OF MATTHEW, MARK, LUKE, AND JESUS

We call Matthew, Mark, and Luke the "Synoptics," because they share so much material in common that ancient readers found that their many similar passages could be compared "at a glance"—which is what the Greek word "synoptic" means. Still, each evangelist has a characteristic style and viewpoint that distinguishes him from his fellows. Mark is the roughest and most primitive, and he recounts the clash between Jesus and the religious establishment of his day in the starkest, least nuanced terms. He also gives us the fewest sayings of Jesus, making his the shortest gospel. Matthew's Greek is better than Mark's, but stiffer and more formal. He is intent on writing correctly, which gives his narrative a certain blandness (at least in contrast to the others). Luke is a delight: he writes a supple, living Greek; he is unafraid to depart from formulas and strictures that had been handed down to him by the previous oral tradition; he knows how to set a scene and shape a story. He is also the most diligent of the Synoptics in turning up great stories (such as the Good Samaritan, the Prodigal Son, the Pharisee and the Publican, Jesus' encounter with his friends Martha and Mary, and his mysterious appearance on the road to Emmaus) that escaped the others. Luke may be the only gentile among the evangelists—perhaps the only gentile among all the authors of the Bible—so it is possible that he was more at ease in Greek than the others were.

In all three evangelists, Jesus behaves in essentially the same way. If Mark's Jesus seems occasionally wild-eyed and Matthew's Jesus raises the occasional yawn on account of his sheer evenness and Luke's Jesus seems on occasion to have a twinkle in his eye, we can pretty much chalk these differences up to the lens of individual personality that each writer brings to his subject, as well as to their unequal literary skills. But all three are manifestly reporting—like three newspaper reporters of very different temperaments—on a fourth man: a man whose personality is almost the whole point of the story they have to tell.

For into the hubbub of first-century Palestine walked a man whom others found instantly attractive, a man who (as no other in their experience had ever done) "spoke with authority," a man one instinctively wanted to follow. This phenomenon of Jesus' personality was no less unusual for **141**

Palestinian Jews of the first century than it would be for us today. Everyone found Jesus remarkable, and it is with this mysterious, unaccountable attraction that the story of Jesus begins.

When he spoke, he did not dispel the mystery. If anything, his words made the mystery deepen. Though his inexplicable magnetism attracted crowds, to whom he told stories that were open to ambiguous interpretation, some found him more and more opaque, and gradually turned away. Others found their hopes growing: this could only be the Messiah—God's Anointed Messenger, come at last as the Jewish scriptures had foretold, to raise them up and scatter their enemies. Still others found their worst suspicions confirmed by the deviousness of his slippery tongue: here was a real troublemaker, who must be got rid of before he invited Roman intervention and involved them all in some bloody political catastrophe.

In our world, worries about the Romans may appear quaint and distant. But we have only to remind ourselves of contemporary freedom movements (such as the American civil rights movement, the movement of indigenous peoples in Latin America, the antiapartheid movement in South **142** Africa, the Solidarity movement in Poland, the free-speech movement in

China) to imagine how terrifying political realities can be. And in such cases, the religious establishment can easily be tempted to side with the dominant political power against those who would upset the applecart.

It has long been Christian custom to dramatize the events leading to Jesus' crucifixion in the week before Easter. In such dramatizations, the part of the crowd of the Jews who urged that Jesus be crucified is usually taken by the congregation, who shout at stated intervals: "Crucify him! Crucify him!" To find oneself among this crowd is to understand that one is, that all of us are—in some cosmic sense—responsible for Jesus' crucifixion. But the church exhibits a certain blindness when it assigns the role of Christ to a local clergyman. Rather, the local clergy should play the Chief Priests of the Jews—the religious establishment—and thus serve as a yearly reminder of the corruption of power and position. A local political figure should be invited to play Pilate to similar effect.

The role of Jesus should be assigned to an outcast. The local beggar, the local prostitute, the local madman, the local illegal alien would all make better candidates than the local priest. Jesus may not have begun as an outcast, but he certainly ended as one. And it was with outcasts that he identified. He told us to look for him not in churches but among the poor and the dispossessed. He told us—he tells us—that he has come not to call the righteous but sinners, you and me. The keynote of Jesus' personality is his compassion—his superhuman ability to suffer with others and for others. Throughout his life, as dramatized by the gospels, his affection and sympathy for children, "for those who mourn," for those publicly accused, for those who hurt on behalf of others, for all those who are somehow bereft, is boundless.

This is the same life he calls us to. This is his invitation.

THE WORDS OF JESUS

From John's Gospel

JESUS IS THE LADDER BETWEEN HEAVEN AND EARTH

> "In all truth I tell you, you will see heaven open and the angels of
> God ascending and descending over the Son of man."
>
> JOHN 1:51

In Genesis 28, Jacob, the grandson of Abraham, has a dream in which he sees a ladder, planted in the earth but reaching to heaven, on which God's angels ascend and descend. Here, Jesus proclaims himself the conduit between human beings and God.

YOU MUST BE BORN AGAIN

> "In all truth I tell you,
> no one can see the kingdom of God
> without being born from above."
>
> JOHN 3:3

A BAPTISMAL INSTRUCTION

> "In all truth I tell you,
> no one can enter the kingdom of God
> without being born through water and the Spirit;
> what is born of human nature is human;
> what is born of the Spirit is spirit.
> Do not be surprised when I say:
> You must be born from above.
> The wind blows where it pleases;
> you can hear its sound,
> but you cannot tell where it comes from or where it is going.
> So it is with everyone who is born of the Spirit."
>
> JOHN 3:5–8

JESUS IS THE HEALING EMBLEM

"No one has gone up to heaven
except the one who came down from heaven,
the Son of man;
as Moses lifted up the snake in the desert,
so must the Son of man be lifted up
so that everyone who believes may have eternal life in him."

JOHN 3:13–15

The snake in the desert is a reference to the brazen serpent (of Numbers 21) that Moses lifted up. All who looked on it were delivered from death by poison. Jesus is alluding obliquely to his being lifted up on the cross (and, afterward, back into the heavens), by which exaltation he will provide healing for all.

GOD SO LOVED THE WORLD

"For this is how God loved the world:
he gave his only Son,
so that everyone who believes in him may not perish
but may have eternal life.
For God sent his Son into the world
not to judge the world,
but so that through him the world might be saved.
No one who believes in him will be judged;
but whoever does not believe is judged already,
because that person does not believe
in the Name of God's only Son.
And the judgment is this:
though the light has come into the world
people have preferred
darkness to the light
because their deeds were evil.

And indeed, everybody who does wrong
hates the light and avoids it,
to prevent his actions from being shown up;
but whoever does the truth
comes out into the light,
so that what he is doing may plainly appear as done in God."

JOHN 3:16–21

JESUS AT JACOB'S WELL

When a Samaritan woman came to draw water, Jesus said to her,
"Give me something to drink." His disciples had gone into the
town to buy food. The Samaritan woman said to him, "You are a
Jew. How is it that you ask me, a Samaritan, for something to
drink?"—Jews, of course, do not associate with Samaritans. Jesus
replied to her:

> "If you only knew what God is offering
> and who it is that is saying to you,
> 'Give me something to drink,'
> you would have been the one to ask,
> and he would have given you living water."

"You have no bucket, sir," she answered, "and the well is deep: how do you get this living water? Are you a greater man than our father Jacob, who gave us this well and drank from it himself with his sons and his cattle?" Jesus replied:

> "Whoever drinks this water
> will be thirsty again;
> but no one who drinks the water that I shall give him
> will ever be thirsty again:
> the water that I shall give him
> will become in him a spring of water, welling up for eternal life."

"Sir," said the woman, "give me some of that water, so that I may never be thirsty or come here again to draw water." "Go and call your husband," said Jesus to her, "and come back here." The woman answered, "I have no husband." Jesus said to her, "You are right to say, 'I have no husband'; for although you have had five, the one you now have is not your husband. You spoke the truth there."

JOHN 4:7–18

WORSHIP IN THE SPIRIT

"I see you are a prophet, sir," said the woman. "Our fathers worshipped on this mountain, though you say that Jerusalem is the place where one ought to worship." Jesus said:

> "Believe me, woman, the hour is coming
> when you will worship the Father

neither on this mountain nor in Jerusalem.
You worship what you do not know;
we worship what we do know;
for salvation comes from the Jews.
But the hour is coming—indeed is already here—
when true worshippers will worship the Father in spirit
    and truth:
that is the kind of worshipper
the Father seeks.
God is spirit,
and those who worship
must worship in spirit and truth."

JOHN 4:19–24

THE TIME IS RIPE

"Do you not have a saying:
Four months and then the harvest?
Well, I tell you,
look around you, look at the fields;
already they are white, ready for harvest!
Already the reaper is being paid his wages,
already he is bringing in the grain for eternal life,
so that sower and reaper can rejoice together.
For here the proverb holds true:
one sows, another reaps;
I sent you to reap
a harvest you have not labored for.

Others have labored for it;
and you have come into the rewards of their labor."

JOHN 4:35-38

THE FATHER WORKS THROUGH HIS SON

"In all truth I tell you,
by himself the Son can do nothing;
he can do only what he sees the Father doing:
and whatever the Father does the Son does too.
For the Father loves the Son
and shows him everything he himself does,
and he will show him even greater things than these,
works that will astonish you.
Thus, as the Father raises the dead and gives them life,
so the Son gives life to anyone he chooses;
for the Father judges no one;

he has entrusted all judgment to the Son,
so that all may honor the Son
as they honor the Father.
Whoever refuses honor to the Son
refuses honor to the Father who sent him."

JOHN 5:19–23

EVEN THE DEAD SHALL LIVE

"In all truth I tell you,
the hour is coming—indeed it is already here—
when the dead will hear the voice of the Son of God,
and all who hear it will live.
For as the Father has life in himself,
so he has granted the Son also to have life in himself;
and, because he is the Son of man,
has granted him power to give judgment.

Do not be surprised at this,
for the hour is coming
when the dead will leave their graves
at the sound of his voice:
those who did good
will come forth to life;
and those who did evil will come forth to judgment."

JOHN 5:25–29

ETERNAL NOURISHMENT

"Do not work for food that goes bad,
but work for food that endures for eternal life,
which the Son of man will give you,
for on him the Father, God himself, has set his seal. . . .
I am the bread of life.

157

No one who comes to me will ever hunger;
no one who believes in me will ever thirst."

JOHN 6:27; 35

JESUS WILL NOT LOSE ANY OF US

"But, as I have told you,
you can see me and still you do not believe.
Everyone whom the Father gives me will come to me;
I will certainly not reject
anyone who comes to me,
because I have come from heaven,
not to do my own will,
but to do the will of him who sent me.
Now the will of him who sent me
is that I should lose nothing
of all that he has given to me,

but that I should raise it up on the last day.
It is my Father's will
that whoever sees the Son and believes in him
should have eternal life,
and that I should raise that person up on the last day."

JOHN 6:36–40

A EUCHARISTIC INSTRUCTION

"In all truth I tell you,
if you do not eat the flesh of the Son of man
and drink his blood,
you have no life in you.
Anyone who does eat my flesh and drink my blood
has eternal life,
and I shall raise that person up on the last day.
For my flesh is real food

159

and my blood is real drink.
Whoever eats my flesh and drinks my blood
lives in me
and I live in that person.
As the living Father sent me
and I draw life from the Father,
so whoever eats me will also draw life from me.
This is the bread which has come down from heaven;
it is not like the bread our ancestors ate:
they are dead,
but anyone who eats this bread will live for ever."

JOHN 6:53–58

This is a reference to the rite, practiced among the early Christians, of consuming bread and wine as the body and blood of Christ. The rite, called the Eucharist or Thanksgiving, goes today under different names in different Christian churches—the Liturgy, the Mass, Communion, and the Lord's Supper.

ONLY THE SPIRIT GIVES LIFE

> "It is the spirit that gives life,
> the flesh has nothing to offer.
> The words I have spoken to you are spirit
> and they are life."

JOHN 6:63

DO NOT JUDGE BY APPEARANCES

"Moses ordered you to practice circumcision—not that it began with him, it goes back to the patriarchs—and you circumcise on the Sabbath. Now if someone can be circumcised on the Sabbath so that the Law of Moses is not broken, why are you angry with me for making someone completely healthy on a Sabbath? Do not

keep judging according to appearances; let your judgment be
according to what is right."

JOHN 7:22–24

JESUS PROMISES LIVING WATER

On the last day, the great day of the festival, Jesus stood and
cried out:

> "Let anyone who is thirsty come to me!
> Let anyone who believes in me come and drink!

As scripture says, 'From his heart shall flow streams of living water.' "
He was speaking of the Spirit which those who believed in
him were to receive; for there was no Spirit as yet because Jesus
had not yet been glorified.

162

JOHN 7:37–39

JESUS DOES NOT CONDEMN

At daybreak he appeared in the Temple again; and as all the people came to him, he sat down and began to teach them.

The scribes and Pharisees brought a woman along who had been caught committing adultery; and making her stand there in the middle they said to Jesus, "Master, this woman was caught in the very act of committing adultery, and in the Law Moses has ordered us to stone women of this kind. What have you got to say?" They asked him this as a test, looking for an accusation to use against him. But Jesus bent down and started writing on the ground with his finger. As they persisted with their question, he straightened up and said, "Let the one among you who is guiltless be the first to throw a stone at her." Then he bent down and continued writing on the ground. When they heard this they went away one by one, beginning with the eldest, until the last one had gone and Jesus was left alone with the woman, who remained in the middle. Jesus again straightened up and said,

163

"Woman, where are they? Has no one condemned you?" "No one, sir," she replied. "Neither do I condemn you," said Jesus. "Go away, and from this moment sin no more."

JOHN 8:2–11

THE LIGHT OF THE WORLD

"I am the light of the world;
anyone who follows me will not be walking in the dark,
but will have the light of life."

JOHN 8:12

THE LIFTING UP OF THE SON OF MAN

"When you have lifted up the Son of man,
then you will know that I am He

and that I do nothing of my own accord.
What I say
is what the Father has taught me;
he who sent me is with me,
and has not left me to myself,
for I always do what pleases him."

JOHN 8:28–29

"MY WORD IS YOUR HOME"

"If you make my word your home
you will indeed be my disciples;
you will come to know the truth,
and the truth will set you free."

JOHN 8:31–32

SIN IS THE ONLY SLAVERY

> "In all truth I tell you,
> everyone who commits sin is a slave.
> Now a slave has no permanent standing in the household,
> but a son belongs to it for ever.
> So if the Son sets you free,
> you will indeed be free."

JOHN 8:34–36

JESUS CROSSES THE LINE

> "Your father Abraham rejoiced
> to think that he would see my Day;
> he saw it and was glad."

The Jews then said, "You are not fifty yet, and you have seen Abraham!" Jesus replied:

> "In all truth I tell you,
> before Abraham ever was,
> I am."

At this they picked up stones to throw at him; but Jesus hid himself and left the Temple.

JOHN 8:56–59

By saying "I am" rather than "I was" (as one would expect), John's Jesus asserts his eternal existence: he is, like God, always present. But to a Jewish ear, he also applies to himself a form of God's holy name, echoing God's words in the prophet Isaiah ("I am he")—and is therefore guilty of the vilest blasphemy and worthy of stoning.

THE CASE OF THE MAN BORN BLIND

As he went along, he saw a man who had been blind from birth. His disciples asked him, "Rabbi, who sinned, this man or his parents, that he should have been born blind?" "Neither he nor his parents sinned," Jesus answered, "he was born blind so that the works of God might be revealed in him.

> As long as day lasts
> we must carry out the work of the one who sent me;
> the night will soon be here when no one can work.
> As long as I am in the world
> I am the light of the world."

Having said this, he spat on the ground, made a paste with the spittle, put this over the eyes of the blind man, and said to him, "Go and wash in the Pool of Siloam" (the name means "one who has been sent"). So he went off and washed and came back able to see.

JOHN 9:1–7

EVER SINCE THE WORLD BEGAN . . .

His neighbors and the people who used to see him before (for he was a beggar) said, "Isn't this the man who used to sit and beg?" Some said, "Yes, it is the same one." Others said, "No, but he looks just like him." The man himself said, "Yes, I am the one." So they said to him, "Then how is it that your eyes were opened?" He answered, "The man called Jesus made a paste, daubed my eyes with it and said to me, 'Go off and wash at Siloam'; so I went, and when I washed I gained my sight." They asked, "Where is he?" He answered, "I don't know."

They brought to the Pharisees the man who had been blind. It had been a Sabbath day when Jesus made the paste and opened the man's eyes, so when the Pharisees asked him how he had gained his sight, he said, "He put a paste on my eyes, and I washed, and I can see." Then some of the Pharisees said, "That man cannot be from God: he does not keep the Sabbath." Others said, "How can a sinner produce signs like this?" And there was division among them. So they spoke to the blind man again, "What have you to say about him yourself, now that he has opened your eyes?" The man answered, "He is a prophet."

However, the Jews would not believe that the man had been blind without first sending for the parents of the man who had gained his sight and asking them, "Is this man really the son of yours who you say was born blind? If so, how is it that he is now able to see?" His parents answered, "We know he is our son and we know he was born blind, but how he can see, we don't know, nor who opened his eyes. Ask him. He is old enough: let him speak for himself." His parents spoke like this out of fear of the Jews, who had already agreed to ban from the synagogue anyone who should acknowledge Jesus as the Christ. This was why his parents said, "He is old enough; ask him."

So the Jews sent for the man again and said to him, "Give glory to God! We are satisfied that this man is a sinner." The man answered, "Whether he is a sinner I don't know; all I know is that I was blind and now I can see." They said to him, "What did he do to you? How did he open your eyes?" He replied, "I have told you once and you wouldn't listen. Why do you want to hear it all again? Do you want to become his disciples yourselves?" At this they hurled abuse at him, "It is you who are his disciple, we are disciples of Moses: we know that God spoke to Moses, but as for this man, we don't know where he comes from." The man replied, "That is just what is so amazing! You don't know where he comes from and he has opened my eyes!

We know that God doesn't listen to sinners, but God does listen to men who are devout and do his will. Ever since the world began it is unheard of for anyone to open the eyes of a man who was born blind; if this man were not from God, he wouldn't have been able to do anything." They retorted, "Are you trying to teach us, and you a sinner through and through ever since you were born!" And they ejected him.

JOHN 9:8–34

THAT THOSE WITHOUT SIGHT MAY SEE

Jesus heard they had ejected him, and when he found him he said to him, "Do you believe in the Son of man?" "Sir," the man replied, "tell me who he is so that I may believe in him." Jesus said, "You have seen him; he is speaking to you." The man said, "Lord, I believe," and worshiped him.

Jesus said:

"It is for judgment
that I have come into this world,
so that those without sight may see
and those with sight may become blind."

Hearing this, some Pharisees who were present said to him, "So we are blind, are we?" Jesus replied:

"If you were blind,
you would not be guilty,
but since you say, 'We can see,'
your guilt remains."

JOHN 9:35–41

THE GOOD SHEPHERD

"I am the good shepherd:
the good shepherd lays down his life for his sheep.
The hired man, since he is not the shepherd
and the sheep do not belong to him,
abandons the sheep
as soon as he sees a wolf coming, and runs away,
and then the wolf attacks and scatters the sheep;
he runs away because he is only a hired man
and has no concern for the sheep.
I am the good shepherd;
I know my own
and my own know me,
just as the Father knows me
and I know the Father;
and I lay down my life for my sheep."

JOHN 10:11–15

THE SHEPHERD MUST BRING HIS SHEEP
TOGETHER FROM MANY FOLDS

"And there are other sheep I have
that are not of this fold,
and I must lead these too.
They too will listen to my voice,
and there will be only one flock,
one shepherd."

JOHN 10:16

"One flock" may be an expression of desire on the part of the writer that the contentions and separations of the early churches end in unity.

THE FATHER LOVES THE SON

> "The Father loves me,
> because I lay down my life
> in order to take it up again.
> No one takes it from me;
> I lay it down of my own free will,
> and as I have power to lay it down,
> so I have power to take it up again;
> and this is the command I have received from my Father."

JOHN 10:17–18

THE SON LOVES US

Jesus loved Martha and her sister and Lazarus, yet when he heard that he was ill he stayed where he was for two more days before saying to the disciples, "Let us go back to Judaea."

He said that and then added, "Our friend Lazarus is at rest; I am going to wake him." The disciples said to him, "Lord, if he is at rest he will be saved." Jesus was speaking of the death of Lazarus, but they thought that by "rest" he meant "sleep"; so Jesus put it plainly, "Lazarus is dead; and for your sake I am glad I was not there because now you will believe. But let us go to him." Then Thomas—known as the Twin—said to the other disciples, "Let us also go to die with him."

On arriving, Jesus found that Lazarus had been in the tomb for four days already. Bethany is only about two miles from Jerusalem, and many Jews had come to Martha and Mary to comfort them about their brother. When Martha heard that Jesus was coming she went to meet him. Mary remained sitting in the house. Martha said to Jesus, "Lord, if you had been here, my brother would not have died, but even now I know that God will grant whatever you ask of him." Jesus said to her, "Your brother will rise again." Martha said, "I know he will rise again at the resurrection on the last day." Jesus said:

"I am the resurrection.
Anyone who believes in me, even though that person dies,
    will live,
and whoever lives and believes in me
will never die.
Do you believe this?"

"Yes, Lord," she said, "I believe that you are the Christ, the Son of God, the one who was to come into this world."

When she had said this, she went and called her sister Mary, saying in a low voice, "The Master is here and wants to see you." Hearing this, Mary got up quickly and went to him. Jesus had not yet come into the village; he was still at the place where Martha had met him. When the Jews who were in the house comforting Mary saw her get up so quickly and go out, they followed her, thinking that she was going to the tomb to weep there.

Mary went to Jesus, and as soon as she saw him she threw
178 herself at his feet, saying, "Lord, if you had been here, my brother

would not have died." At the sight of her tears, and those of the Jews who had come with her, Jesus was greatly distressed, and with a profound sigh he said, "Where have you put him?" They said, "Lord, come and see." Jesus wept; and the Jews said, "See how much he loved him!"

JOHN 11:5–7; 11–36

JESUS "WAKENS" LAZARUS

But there were some who remarked, "He opened the eyes of the blind man. Could he not have prevented this man's death?" Sighing again, Jesus reached the tomb: it was a cave with a stone to close the opening. Jesus said, "Take the stone away." Martha, the dead man's sister, said to him, "Lord, by now he

179

will smell; this is the fourth day since he died." Jesus replied, "Have I not told you that if you believe you will see the glory of God?" So they took the stone away. Then Jesus lifted up his eyes and said:

"Father, I thank you for hearing my prayer.
I myself knew that you hear me always,
but I speak
for the sake of all these who are standing around me,
so that they may believe it was you who sent me."

When he had said this, he cried in a loud voice, "Lazarus, come out!" The dead man came out, his feet and hands bound with strips of material, and a cloth over his face. Jesus said to them, "Unbind him, let him go free."

JOHN 11:37–44

JESUS IS ANOINTED

Six days before the Passover, Jesus went to Bethany, where Lazarus was, whom he had raised from the dead. They gave a dinner for him there; Martha waited on them and Lazarus was among those at table. Mary brought in a pound of very costly ointment, pure nard, and with it anointed the feet of Jesus, wiping them with her hair; the house was filled with the scent of the ointment. Then Judas Iscariot—one of his disciples, the man who was to betray him—said, "Why was this ointment not sold for three hundred denarii and the money given to the poor?" He said this, not because he cared about the poor, but because he was a thief; he was in charge of the common fund and used to help himself to the contents. So Jesus said, "Leave her alone; let her keep it for the day of my burial. You have the poor with you always, you will not always have me."

JOHN 12:1–8

This is John's version of the incident. Matthew's was given earlier (on pages 119–120). Mark's is virtually identical to Matthew's. Luke omits the incident, perhaps because his gentile audience would not have grasped the significance of anointing. John is more particular than Matthew. He identifies the woman as Mary of Bethany (not Mary Magdalene, as would be thought in later times) and the complainer as Judas Iscariot. This vignette of Judas gives us, incidentally, the sharpest insight we have into his character. John is also more sensual: the hair, the scent. But Mary anoints not Jesus' head (as in Matthew and as might be expected), but his feet: John's Jesus is just too august for anyone to touch his head. These details give a good indication of the differences between John and the Synoptics: John is often more precise, full of details that could only have come originally from a perceptive eyewitness with firsthand knowledge of Jewish life; but his Jesus is on his way to becoming an icon and lacks the sinewy elasticity of the Synoptic Jesus.

LIFE FROM DEATH

"In all truth I tell you,
unless a wheat grain falls into the earth and dies,
it remains only a single grain;
but if it dies
it yields a rich harvest.
Anyone who loves his life loses it;
anyone who hates his life in this world
will keep it for eternal life.
Whoever serves me, must follow me,
and my servant will be with me wherever I am.
If anyone serves me, my Father will honor him."

JOHN 12:24–26

183

GOOD OVER EVIL

"Now sentence is being passed on this world;
now the prince of this world is to be driven out.
And when I am lifted up from the earth,
I shall draw all people to myself."

JOHN 12:30–32

"The prince of this world" is Satan.

JESUS, THE IMAGE OF GOD, WASHES THE FEET OF OTHERS

Jesus knew that the Father had put everything into his hands,
and that he had come from God and was returning to God, and
he got up from table, removed his outer garments and, taking a
towel, wrapped it round his waist; he then poured water into a

basin and began to wash the disciples' feet and to wipe them with the towel he was wearing.

He came to Simon Peter, who said to him, "Lord, are you going to wash my feet?" Jesus answered, "At the moment you do not know what I am doing, but later you will understand." "Never!" said Peter, "You shall never wash my feet." Jesus replied, "If I do not wash you, you can have no share with me." Simon Peter said, "Well then, Lord, not only my feet, but my hands and my head as well!" . . .

When he had washed their feet and put on his outer garments again he went back to the table. "Do you understand," he said, "what I have done to you? You call me Master and Lord, and rightly; so I am. If I, then, the Lord and Master, have washed your feet, you must wash each other's feet. I have given you an example so that you may copy what I have done to you."

JOHN 13:3–9; 12–15

Having said this, Jesus was deeply disturbed and declared, "In all truth I tell you, one of you is going to betray me." The disciples looked at each other, wondering whom he meant. The disciple Jesus loved was reclining next to Jesus; Simon Peter signed to him and said, "Ask who it is he means," so leaning back close to Jesus' chest he said, "Who is it, Lord?" Jesus answered, "It is the one to whom I give the piece of bread that I dip in the dish." And when he had dipped the piece of bread he gave it to Judas son of Simon Iscariot. At that instant, after Judas had taken the bread, Satan entered him. Jesus then said, "What you are going to do, do quickly." None of the others at table understood why he said this. Since Judas had charge of the common fund, some of them thought Jesus was telling him, "Buy what we need for the festival," or telling him to give something to the poor. As soon as Judas had taken the piece of bread he went out. It was night.

JOHN 13:21–30

THE NEW COMMANDMENT

"I give you a new commandment:
love one another;
you must love one another
just as I have loved you.
It is by your love for one another,
that everyone will recognize you
as my disciples."

JOHN 13:34–35

THE WAY

Thomas said, "Lord, we do not know where you are going, so how
can we know the way?" Jesus said:

"I am the Way; I am Truth and Life.
No one can come to the Father except through me.
If you know me, you will know my Father too.
From this moment you know him and have seen him."

JOHN 14:5–7

THE FAMILY OF LOVE

"If you love me you will keep my commandments.
I shall ask the Father,
and he will give you another Paraclete
to be with you for ever,
the Spirit of truth
whom the world can never accept

since it neither sees nor knows him;
but you know him,
because he is with you, he is in you.
I shall not leave you orphans;
I shall come to you.
In a short time the world will no longer see me;
but you will see that I live
and you also will live.
On that day
you will know that I am in my Father
and you in me and I in you.
Whoever holds to my commandments and keeps them
is the one who loves me;
and whoever loves me will be loved by my Father,
and I shall love him and reveal myself to him."

JOHN 14:15–21

GOD'S SPIRIT WILL LIVE IN US

"I have said these things to you
while still with you;
but the Paraclete, the Holy Spirit,
whom the Father will send in my name,
will teach you everything
and remind you of all I have said to you."

JOHN 14:25–26

THE PEACE OF CHRIST

"Peace I bequeath to you,
my own peace I give you,
a peace which the world cannot give, this is my gift to you.
Do not let your hearts be troubled or afraid."

JOHN 14:27

THE TRUE VINE

"I am the true vine,
and my Father is the vinedresser.
Every branch in me that bears no fruit
he cuts away,
and every branch that does bear fruit he prunes
to make it bear even more.
You are clean already,
by means of the word that I have spoken to you.
Remain in me, as I in you.
As a branch cannot bear fruit all by itself,
unless it remains part of the vine,
neither can you unless you remain in me.
I am the vine,
you are the branches.
Whoever remains in me, with me in him,
bears fruit in plenty;

for cut off from me you can do nothing.
Anyone who does not remain in me
is thrown away like a branch
—and withers;
these branches are collected and thrown on the fire,
and are burnt.
If you remain in me
and my words remain in you,
you may ask for whatever you please
and you will get it.
It is to the glory of my Father that you should bear much fruit,
and be my disciples."

JOHN 15:1–8

WHY JESUS TELLS US THIS

"I have loved you
just as the Father has loved me.
Remain in my love.
If you keep my commandments
you will remain in my love,
just as I have kept my Father's commandments
and remain in his love.
I have told you this
so that my own joy may be in you
and your joy be complete."

JOHN 15:9–11

THE GREATEST LOVE

"This is my commandment:
love one another,
as I have loved you.
No one can have greater love
than to lay down his life for his friends."

JOHN 15:12–13

WE ARE NO LONGER SERVANTS, BUT FRIENDS

"You are my friends,
if you do what I command you.
I shall no longer call you servants,
because a servant does not know
his master's business;
I call you friends,

because I have made known to you
everything I have learned from my Father.
You did not choose me,
no, I chose you;
and I commissioned you
to go out and to bear fruit,
fruit that will last;
so that the Father will give you
anything you ask him in my name.
My command to you
is to love one another."

JOHN 15:14–17

EXPECT PERSECUTION

"If the world hates you,
you must realize that it hated me before it hated you.

If you belonged to the world,
the world would love you as its own;
but because you do not belong to the world,
because my choice of you has drawn you out of the world,
that is why the world hates you.
Remember the words I said to you:
A servant is not greater than his master.
If they persecuted me,
they will persecute you too;
if they kept my word,
they will keep yours as well.
But it will be on my account that they will do all this to you,
because they do not know the one who sent me."

JOHN 15:18–21

JESUS PRAYS TO HIS FATHER

"May they all be one,
just as, Father, you are in me and I am in you,
so that they also may be in us,
so that the world may believe it was you who sent me.
I have given them the glory you gave to me,
that they may be one as we are one.
With me in them and you in me,
may they be so perfected in unity
that the world will recognize that it was you who sent me
and that you have loved them as you loved me."

JOHN 17:21–23

LOVE BEFORE THE FOUNDATION OF THE WORLD

"Father,
I want those you have given me
to be with me where I am,
so that they may always see my glory
which you have given me
because you loved me
before the foundation of the world.
Father, Upright One,
the world has not known you,
but I have known you,
and these have known
that you have sent me.

I have made your name known to them
and will continue to make it known,
so that the love with which you loved me may be in them,
and so that I may be in them."

JOHN 17:24–26

JESUS BEFORE PILATE

Jesus replied, "Mine is not a kingdom of this world; if my
kingdom were of this world, my men would have fought to
prevent my being surrendered to the Jews. As it is, my kingdom
does not belong here." Pilate said, "So, then you are a king?"
Jesus answered, "It is you who say that I am a king. I was born for
this, I came into the world for this, to bear witness to the truth;
and all who are on the side of truth listen to my voice." "Truth?"
said Pilate. "What is that?"

JOHN 18:36–38

"WHERE DO YOU COME FROM?"

Re-entering the Praetorium, he said to Jesus, "Where do you come from?" But Jesus made no answer. Pilate then said to him, "Are you refusing to speak to me? Surely you know I have power to release you and I have power to crucify you?" Jesus replied, "You would have no power over me at all if it had not been given you from above; that is why the one who handed me over to you has the greater guilt."

JOHN 19:9–11

MOTHER AND SON

Near the cross of Jesus stood his mother and his mother's sister, Mary the wife of Clopas, and Mary of Magdala. Seeing his mother and the disciple whom he loved standing near her, Jesus said to his mother, "Woman, this is your son." Then to the disciple he said, "This is your mother." And from that hour the disciple took her into his home.

JOHN 19:25–27

JESUS DIES

After this, Jesus knew that everything had now been completed and, so that the scripture should be completely fulfilled, he said:
> *"I am thirsty."*

A jar full of sour wine stood there; so, putting a sponge soaked in the wine on a hyssop stick, they held it up to his mouth. After Jesus had taken the wine he said, "It is fulfilled," and bowing his head he gave up his spirit.

JOHN 19:28–30

THE PIERCED MESSIAH

It was the Day of Preparation, and to avoid the bodies' remaining on the cross during the Sabbath—since that Sabbath was a day of special solemnity—the Jews asked Pilate to have the legs broken and the bodies taken away. Consequently the soldiers came and broke the legs of the first man who had been crucified with him and then of the other. When they came to Jesus, they saw he was already dead, and so instead of breaking his legs one of the soldiers pierced his side with a lance; and immediately there came out blood and water. This is the evidence of one who saw it—true evidence, and he knows that what he says is true—and he gives it so that you may believe as well. Because all this happened to fulfill the words of scripture:

Not one bone of his will be broken;

and again, in another place scripture says:

They will look to the one whom they have pierced.

JOHN 19:31–37

In the churches of the early centuries, the effusions of blood and water were taken as emblems of the principal sacraments of baptism (water) and eucharist (blood), signifying that thus did the Church, the new Eve, issue from the side of Christ, the new Adam who brought us to salvation, just as the first Eve had once issued from the side of the first Adam, who brought us to damnation. See also John 7:38–39.

JUST BEFORE DAWN

It was very early on the first day of the week and still dark, when Mary of Magdala came to the tomb. She saw that the stone had been moved away from the tomb and came running to Simon Peter and the other disciple, the one whom Jesus loved. "They have taken the Lord out of the tomb," she said, "and we don't know where they have put him."

So Peter set out with the other disciple to go to the tomb. They ran together, but the other disciple, running faster than Peter, reached the tomb first; he bent down and saw the linen cloths lying on the ground, but did not go in. Simon Peter, following him, also came up, went into the tomb, saw the linen cloths lying on the ground and also the cloth that had been over his head; this was not with the linen cloths but rolled up in a place by itself. Then the other disciple who had reached the tomb first also went in; he saw and he believed. Till this moment they had still not understood the scripture, that he must rise from the dead. The disciples then went back home.

JOHN 20:1–10

THE FIRST APPEARANCE OF THE RISEN JESUS

But Mary was standing outside near the tomb, weeping. Then, as she wept, she stooped to look inside, and saw two angels in white sitting where the body of Jesus had been, one at the head, the other at the feet. They said, "Woman, why are you weeping?" "They have taken my Lord away," she replied, "and I don't know where they have put him." As she said this she turned round and saw Jesus standing there, though she did not realize that it was Jesus. Jesus said to her, "Woman, why are you weeping? Who are you looking for?" Supposing him to be the gardener, she said, "Sir, if you have taken him away, tell me where you have put him, and I will go and remove him." Jesus said, "Mary!" She turned round then and said to him in Hebrew, "Rabbuni!"—which means Master. Jesus said to her, "Do not cling to me, because I have not yet ascended to the Father. But go and find my brothers, and tell them: I am ascending to my Father and your Father, to my God and your God." So Mary of

Magdala told the disciples, "I have seen the Lord," and that he
had said these things to her.

JOHN 20:11–18

*John's assertion that Jesus appeared to the penitent Mary Magdalene before he appeared
to any of the "brothers" and that he commissioned her to "tell them" gave her the unique
title in subsequent Christian tradition of "Apostle to the Apostles." But in all four
gospels, women are the first evangelists—that is, the first bearers of the Good News.*

THE RISEN JESUS COMMISSIONS HIS DISCIPLES

> "Peace be with you.
> As the Father sent me,
> so am I sending you."

206

After saying this he breathed on them and said:

"Receive the Holy Spirit.
If you forgive anyone's sins,
they are forgiven;
if you retain anyone's sins,
they are retained."

JOHN 20:21–23

THE RISEN JESUS LOOKS FORWARD TO OUR FAITH IN HIM

Thomas, called the Twin, who was one of the Twelve, was not
with them when Jesus came. So the other disciples said to him,
"We have seen the Lord," but he answered, "Unless I can see the
holes that the nails made in his hands and can put my finger into
the holes they made, and unless I can put my hand into his side, I
refuse to believe." Eight days later the disciples were in the house
again and Thomas was with them. The doors were closed, but
Jesus came in and stood among them. "Peace be with you," he

said. Then he spoke to Thomas, "Put your finger here; look, here are my hands. Give me your hand; put it into my side. Do not be unbelieving any more but believe." Thomas replied, "My Lord and my God!" Jesus said to him:

> "You believe because you can see me.
> Blessed are those who have not seen and yet believe."

JOHN 20:24–29

THE RISEN JESUS COOKS BREAKFAST

Simon Peter, Thomas called the Twin, Nathanael from Cana in Galilee, the sons of Zebedee and two more of his disciples were together. Simon Peter said, "I'm going fishing." They replied,

"We'll come with you." They went out and got into the boat but caught nothing that night.

When it was already light, there stood Jesus on the shore, though the disciples did not realize that it was Jesus. Jesus called out, "Haven't you caught anything, friends?" And when they answered, "No," he said, "Throw the net out to starboard and you'll find something." So they threw the net out and could not haul it in because of the quantity of fish. The disciple whom Jesus loved said to Peter, "It is the Lord." At these words "It is the Lord," Simon Peter tied his outer garment round him (for he had nothing on) and jumped into the water. The other disciples came on in the boat, towing the net with the fish; they were only about a hundred yards from land.

As soon as they came ashore they saw that there was some bread there and a charcoal fire with fish cooking on it. Jesus said, "Bring some of the fish you have just caught." Simon Peter went aboard and dragged the net ashore, full of big fish, one hundred and fifty-three of them; and in spite of there being so many the net was not broken. Jesus said to them, "Come and have breakfast." None of the disciples was bold enough to ask, "Who are you?" They knew quite well it was the Lord. Jesus then stepped forward, took the bread and gave it to them, and the same with the fish. This was the third time that Jesus revealed himself to the disciples after rising from the dead.

JOHN 21:2–14

THE RISEN JESUS COMMISSIONS PETER

When they had eaten, Jesus said to Simon Peter, "Simon son of John, do you love me more than these others do?" He answered, "Yes, Lord, you know I love you." Jesus said to him, "Feed my lambs." A second time he said to him, "Simon son of John, do you love me?" He replied, "Yes, Lord, you know I love you." Jesus said to him, "Look after my sheep." Then he said to him a third time, "Simon son of John, do you love me?" Peter was hurt that he asked him a third time, "Do you love me?" and said, "Lord, you know everything; you know I love you." Jesus said to him, "Feed my sheep.

> In all truth I tell you,
> when you were young
> you put on your own belt
> and walked where you liked;
> but when you grow old
> you will stretch out your hands,
> and somebody else will put a belt round you
> and take you where you would rather not go."

In these words he indicated the kind of death by which Peter
would give glory to God. After this he said, "Follow me."

JOHN 21:15–19

*Peter was crucified (probably upside down in the pleasure gardens of the Emperor
Nero) and buried on Rome's Vatican hill directly beneath what is today the papal
altar of Saint Peter's Basilica.*

THE PROBLEM OF JOHN'S GOSPEL

The fourth gospel is more complex than the other three. Its author is unlikely to have been John the Apostle, who we know was a fisherman on Lake
Tiberias in Galilee. In fact, it is unlikely that this gospel has one author. In
its earliest form, it appears to have been the testimony of a man who called
himself "the beloved disciple" (the fourth gospel never uses the term "apostle" of anyone), who lived in the neighborhood of Jerusalem. We know of his

Jerusalem connection because early in his passion narrative we are given the incidental information that he "was known to the high priest" (John 18:16), which no Galilean fisherman would have been. This "beloved disciple" makes his first appearance late in John's gospel—at the Last Supper, "leaning back close to Jesus' chest" (John 13:23).

But if the fourth gospel's witness to the events of Jesus' life is this anonymous disciple, such a man is unlikely to have been the final editor, that is, the one who put this gospel in the form we have it today. For we find all through this gospel evidence of the increasing acrimony and bitterness between the Jews who believed in Jesus' messiahship and those who did not. And we know that the final parting of the ways between these two communities (which is taken as a done deed in the fourth gospel) did not occur until late in the first century. Tensions there had always been, but for a long time Jewish Christians had continued to worship and maintain fellowship with other Jews. Only by century's end would you find Jewish Christians calling other Jews "the Jews" (as we find in this gospel), as if they were an alien people. So, if we are to assume that the beloved disciple reedited his earlier narrative as an old man in order to take account of new conflicts, we must also assume that he was about a hundred years old when he did so!

The reader may notice that in John's Gospel, Jesus tends to give speeches, rather than offer short sayings. (The effect is diluted in this collection, which, wherever possible, reduces long passages to smaller components for the sake of easy digestibility.) These speeches can often make Jesus sound more solemn than he normally does in the Synoptics, sometimes a little too grand, so that we may find ourselves missing the earthier Jesus of the other gospels. But the lengthening of Jesus' pronouncements has a purpose here: several generations of reflection on the meaning of Jesus' life have yielded a richer, more exacting interpretation of Jesus and his mission. In the other gospels, we encounter the phenomenon of Jesus, as it were, from the outside—in the surprising effect he had on his contemporaries. John presumes to give us a glimpse of Jesus from the inside—from his own perspective as the Word of God come down from heaven.

But John, no less than his fellow evangelists, sees Jesus as lover of mankind—that is, of individual human beings—and healer of those who have lost out. In fact, whatever the background of the author (or authors) of this gospel and whatever his actual connection to Jesus, he exhibits a special courage in regard to this central theme: whereas Matthew shows us that Jesus is to be found among the poor (Matthew 25:31–46) and Luke gives us the Good Samaritan (a despised heretic who succors a mugged man left for dead) as the model for all who would follow Jesus, John allows us to see Jesus' special love of women—throughout human history the form of humanity most consistently marginalized. Though Jesus' equal treatment of women is a feature of all four gospels, John emphasizes it especially. In portraying, for instance, Jesus' response to his mother at Cana (for whom he performs his first miracle, not included in this collection) and to the much-married and not-too-bright Samaritan woman at the well (to whom he offers eternal life), John has the audacity to go beyond the rigid conventions of his time in a way that is particularly refreshing to us today. Jews avoided the heretical Samaritans, and no pious Jewish male would engage a strange woman, heretic or otherwise, in conversation. But Jesus truly offers his life to all—especially those excluded by others.

John's Gospel is instructive to our time in yet another way, for it is at once the most Protestant and the most Catholic of gospels. It is the most

Protestant because of its insight into the personal and subjective aspects of life and because of the importance it places on one's individual response to Jesus—on being "born again." It is the most Catholic because it has the most developed sacramental sense of the four gospels: when Jesus spits on the ground, for instance, and with his own hands makes a mud paste to apply to the eyes of the man born blind (John 9:6), his action has all the earmarks of a Catholic sacrament.

The epilogue of John's Gospel, in which Peter is given the commission to care for Jesus' flock, is often read as a kind of belated submission by the personalist, woman-exalting, structure-ignoring Community of the Beloved Disciple—the community out of which this gospel developed—to the bishop-dominated, structure-loving Great Church, which would become in time the Catholic Church (or, if you view subsequent history from an Eastern perspective, the Orthodox Church). No doubt it is. But, perhaps at a deeper level, it represents a compromise between two tendencies of early Christianity—tendencies that can be used creatively and, in any case, have never gone away. Perhaps it is meant, more than anything else, as a final reminder to those who would follow Jesus that our principal (and only?) obligation is to feed the lambs of God—that is, give nourishment and support to those who need our help.

At any rate, no one—church or individual—can find justification in these gospels. The Orthodox, as well as the Catholic, churches will always be brought up short in their glorification of a professional, hierarchic priesthood by the unambiguous teaching of Jesus in Matthew 23: "Call no one on earth your father." Protestants must always be confounded in their theory of Election when they come upon Matthew 25, in which Jesus clearly makes good works—not faith—the sign of personal salvation.

In a similar manner, each reader will find in these texts both profound comfort and radical criticism. God loves me—without qualification. He sets no bounds to his love (Matthew 5:48), but loves me so much that he sent his only son (John 3:16), who willingly suffered and died for me. But God expects something of me, which I am withholding. Only I know what that is, for it is something only I can provide.

In the end, we all fail to meet the mark, whatever that may be in each individual case. In the end, the only difference between Judas and Peter, both of whom betray Jesus, is that Peter did not despair of God's mercy. This is, similarly, the difference between the Pharisee and the Publican in Luke's account. The Pharisee presumes to justify himself; but the Publican throws himself on the mercy of God. For, as William Langland wrote six centuries ago in his *Vision of Piers Plowman:*

> *All the wickedness in this world that man might work or think*
> *Is no more to the mercy of God than a live coal in the sea.*

In such a thought may lie the resolution to the old faith-versus-works controversy. We are called to love Christ in the marginalized and bereft. That is our commission and principal duty. All are called, whether they know it or not. All must treat these outcasts as they would Christ—even if they don't know Christ, even if they don't perform these healing actions with conscious intent. But we are not Christ, we are Peter—and sooner or later, we will betray him, that is, betray the commission he has given us. It is then that we must divest ourselves of the self-justification of the Pharisee and, naked and foolish, wrap ourselves in the garment of faith—a faith that in the New Testament is often more like faith*fulness* or loyalty than like religious belief. And if, as with Peter, even this proves too difficult to sustain, we have only to keep from the despair of Judas. Like Peter and the Publican, we must all throw ourselves on the mercy of God.

CAN WE TALK ABOUT INSPIRATION?

Are the gospels inspired by God? Well, they were certainly written by human beings, men who had very different personalities and somewhat different priorities—and those differences affected considerably their choice of words, their ability to communicate, and their portraits of Jesus. So, if we imagine inspiration to be a sort of hypnosis during which the writer hears God speaking directly to him and writes down precisely what he hears, the gospels are not inspired.

But such a view ignores the way in which human beings actually receive information. Whether sitting in a lecture hall or watching a movie or making love, each human being receives information differently from anyone else, which is why one student's notes can be so different from another's, one movie critic can so violently disagree with another, one friend can so misunderstand another—even in the most intimate moments. Why should we expect the God who created us to eradicate his creation, to eradicate the filter of individual personality, in this one instance of biblical inspiration?

The gospels are full of personalities: Zacchaeus, too short to see Jesus without climbing a tree; Mrs. Zebedee, misunderstanding everything; Peter, the brash, the bold, the bully, the coward, the remorseful, the steadfast; Mary, the brave and beautiful; cautious Nicodemus who comes to Jesus "by night"; and many others whose characteristic selves may be spotted only by a careful reading of each gospel. Jesus himself had a personality. As we said in commenting on the Synoptics, personality is almost the whole point of the gospels. Jesus appeared as a particular body: tall or short, hairy or smooth, muscular or frail, neat or sloppy, loud or soft, ebullient or contained. The Word of God—that is, what God has to say to us—was made flesh, particular flesh.

We do not, and cannot, receive God abstractly; we must receive him concretely. We should not look for Jesus in thoughts but in the concrete people who come our way. The human gene pool, by which new, unrepeatable, utterly unique human beings come to be, is God's constant miracle and gift to us. By this gene pool came Jesus, who still speaks to us. By this gene pool came the evangelists, who still speak to us of Jesus. Is there inspiration here? "Inspiration" means, literally, the breathing of the Spirit, the animating of what was lifeless. Does the Spirit of God breathe upon this process, this ever-changing dance of humanity? Can we believe otherwise?

Is there inspiration, then, beyond the bounds of the Bible? Yes, for God speaks to us in our hearts (though we must be awfully careful that we are not merely hearing what we want to hear). So even though we grant the gospels—and the larger Bible—privileged rank, we may also say that God's Word is to be found in many places and on many lips. Beyond the gospels and beyond the Bible, one comes occasionally upon passages in literature that seem *truly* inspired: the great prayers of Francis of Assisi ("The Canticle of the Sun" and "Make Me a Channel of Your Peace"), for instance; parts of Dante's *Comedy;* the letters of Jean-Pierre de Caussade, collected under the title *Abandonment to Divine Providence;* the story of "The Grand Inquisitor" in Dostoevsky's *The Brothers Karamazov;* the prison writings of Dietrich Bonhoeffer; C. S. Lewis' *Perelandra.* Even the words of Jesus (some of them, at least, seemingly authentic) may be found outside the gospels.

Two instances are given next: Jesus' words as heard in a vision by the author of Revelation, the mysterious last book of the New Testament; and a fragment, called by scholars Papyrus Oxyrhynchus I, which was found in an Egyptian garbage heap. The saying from Revelation speaks to the end of time, when Jesus shall return: The time may seem interminable to us, but, Jesus assures us, it is not. The saying from the Egyptian fragment speaks to the present, to the place where we find ourselves at this very moment.

WORDS OF JESUS

From Beyond the Gospels

JESUS CHRIST, YESTERDAY, TODAY, AND THE SAME FOREVER

I am indeed coming soon.

REVELATION 22:20

Cleave the wood: I am there. Lift the stone, and you will find me there.

PAPYRUS OXYRHYN-
CHUS I, NO. 30

This Greek fragment is now known to have been part of the so-called Gospel of Thomas, which has since been discovered in its entirety in a third-century Coptic version. It is not a narrative gospel, only a collection of Jesus' sayings edited from a gnostic-pantheistic perspective. It was lost to subsequent generations because the majority of Christians found it unorthodox, and therefore scribes ceased to copy its

225

text. Such heretical collections as we still possess present to us not a Jesus of flesh and blood, but a ghostly, sexually ambivalent figure, whom one could hardly imagine attracting the down-to-earth crowds of first-century Palestine. Still, there remain, even in these peculiar collections, elements of the real Jesus. This fragment is open to a pantheistic interpretation (everything is God/Christ), but it is also open to an orthodox interpretation (God/Christ is everywhere).

PRAYING WITH JESUS

This collection closes with two psalms (which are lyrical prayers, originally set to music). Jesus did not compose these psalms. Rather, they are credited to his remote ancestor King David, who lived a thousand years before him. But we know that Jesus loved these prayers and knew them by heart.

The first, Psalm 22, is echoed in the Magnificat, the psalmlike prayer that Jesus' mother, Mary of Nazareth, spoke on learning that she was to give **226** birth to Jesus (Luke 1:46–55, not in this collection). So we may even suppose that Jesus learned this psalm at his mother's knee. It is, in its entirety, a ringing affirmation that God will work his justice, despite all appearances to the contrary. It should come as no surprise that this would be the prayer that Jesus would hold onto in his most extreme agony, nailed barbarically to a pole and slowly bleeding to death as we saw on page 130. This is a psalm to pray in the worst of times. We may also imagine that this psalm was one of the "passages throughout the scriptures that were about himself" that the risen Jesus explained to the two disciples on the road to Emmaus (Luke 24:27).

The second, Psalm 23, is probably the best-loved passage in the whole of the Bible. We know that Jesus loved it, too, because, in portraying himself as the Good Shepherd (John 10), he built purposely on his audience's familiarity with this psalm, in which God himself is the Good Shepherd. This is a psalm to pray in good times, a psalm to teach to children, a psalm for comfort at nightfall, a psalm to whisper before sleep.

We pray these psalms, knowing that Jesus prayed them and that he made their words his own. They are given here in the sumptuous rendering of the King James Version.

PSALM 22

My God, my God, why hast thou forsaken me? why art thou so far from
    helping me, and from the words of my roaring?
O my God, I cry in the daytime, but thou hearest not; and in the night
    season, and am not silent.
But thou art holy, O thou that inhabitest the praises of Israel.
Our fathers trusted in thee: they trusted, and thou didst deliver them.
They cried unto thee, and were delivered: they trusted in thee, and were not
    confounded.
But I am a worm, and no man; a reproach of men, and despised of the
    people.
All they that see me laugh me to scorn: they shoot out the lip, they shake
    the head, saying,

He trusted on the LORD that he would deliver him: let him deliver him, seeing he delighted in him.

But thou art he that took me out of the womb: thou didst make me hope when I was upon my mother's breasts.

I was cast upon thee from the womb: thou art my God from my mother's belly.

Be not far from me; for trouble is near; for there is none to help.

Many bulls have compassed me: strong bulls of Bashan have beset me round.

They gaped upon me with their mouths, as a ravening and a roaring lion.

I am poured out like water, and all my bones are out of joint: my heart is like wax; it is melted in the midst of my bowels.

My strength is dried up like a potsherd; and my tongue cleaveth to my jaws; and thou hast brought me into the dust of death.

For dogs have compassed me: the assembly of the wicked have inclosed me: they pierced my hands and my feet.

I may tell all my bones: they look and stare upon me.

They part my garments among them, and cast lots upon my vesture.

But be not thou far from me, O LORD: O my strength, haste thee to help me.

Deliver my soul from the sword; my darling from the power of the dog.

Save me from the lion's mouth: for thou hast heard me from the horns of the unicorns.

I will declare thy name unto my brethren: in the midst of the congregation will I praise thee.

Ye that fear the LORD, praise him; all ye the seed of Jacob, glorify him; and fear him, all ye the seed of Israel.

For he hath not despised nor abhorred the affliction of the afflicted; neither hath he hid his face from him; but when he cried unto him, he heard.

My praise shall be of thee in the great congregation: I will pay my vows before them that fear him.

The meek shall eat and be satisfied: they shall praise the LORD that seek him: your heart shall live for ever.

All the ends of the world shall remember and turn unto the LORD: and all the kindreds of the nations shall worship before thee.

230 For the kingdom is the LORD'S: and he is the governor among the nations.

All they that be fat upon earth shall eat and worship: all they that go down
to the dust shall bow before him: and none can keep alive his own soul.
A seed shall serve him; it shall be accounted to the Lord for a generation.
They shall come, and shall declare his righteousness unto a people that shall
be born, that he hath done this.

PSALM 23

The LORD is my shepherd; I shall not want.

He maketh me to lie down in green pastures: he leadeth me beside the still waters.

He restoreth my soul: he leadeth me in the paths of righteousness for his name's sake.

Yea, though I walk through the valley of the shadow of death, I will fear no evil: for thou art with me; thy rod and thy staff they comfort me.

Thou preparest a table before me in the presence of mine enemies: thou anointest my head with oil; my cup runneth over.

Surely goodness and mercy shall follow me all the days of my life: and I will dwell in the house of the LORD for ever.

THEMATIC INDEX

THEMES IN THE GOSPELS OF MATTHEW, MARK, AND LUKE

THEMES IN JOHN'S GOSPEL

ABOUT THE COMPILER

Thomas Cahill studied at New York's Union Theological Seminary, Columbia University, and Fordham University with some of America's most distinguished literary and biblical scholars. He founded The Cahill and Company Catalogue, much beloved by book readers, and is now Director of Religious Publishing at Doubleday. He lives in New York City with his wife, Susan Cahill. They have two children, both at college.